EXPLORING CAREERS

Careers in Aviation and Aerospace

Stuart A. Kallen

ReferencePoint Press®

© 2017 ReferencePoint Press, Inc.
Printed in the United States

For more information, contact:
ReferencePoint Press, Inc.
PO Box 27779
San Diego, CA 92198
www.ReferencePointPress.com

LIBRARY OF CONGRESS CATALOGING-IN-PUBLICATION DATA

Names: Kallen, Stuart A., 1955– author.
Title: Careers in aviation and aerospace / by Stuart A. Kallen.
Description: San Diego, CA : ReferencePoint Press, Inc., 2017. | Series: Exploring careers | Includes bibliographical references and index. | Audience: Grade 9 to 12.
Identifiers: LCCN 2016040555 (print) | LCCN 2016042931 (ebook) | ISBN 9781682821015 (hardback) | ISBN 9781682821039 (eBook)
Subjects: LCSH: Aeronautics--Vocational guidance--Juvenile literature. | Aerospace industries--Vocational guidance--Juvenile literature.
Classification: LCC TL561 .K357 2017 (print) | LCC TL561 (ebook) | DDC 629.13023--dc23
LC record available at https://lccn.loc.gov/2016040555

Contents

Introduction: Shooting for the Stars   4

Aerospace Engineer   8

Aerospace Engineering and Operations Technician   16

Aircraft and Avionics Equipment Mechanic   24

Commercial Pilot   32

Air Traffic Controller   40

Meteorologist   48

Planetary Scientist   56

Astronaut   63

Interview with an Aerospace Engineer   71

Other Careers in Aviation and Aerospace   74

Index   75

Picture Credits   79

About the Author   80

Shooting for the Stars

In 1980, when tech entrepreneur Elon Musk was nine years old, he was so fascinated with outer space that his father encouraged him to build his own rockets. Musk later joked that he somehow managed to keep all his fingers while shooting a variety of hazardous homemade missiles into the sky. In addition to his fingers, Musk kept his love of rockets and outer space intact. Even as Musk's financial service company PayPal made him an Internet billionaire, he studied textbooks with names like *Rocket Propulsion Elements* and *International Reference Guide to Space Launch Systems* in his spare time.

In 2002 Musk founded the space transportation company SpaceX, and within a few years the company set some notable precedents. In 2008 SpaceX became the first privately owned company to launch a rocket into space, and in 2015 the company became the first entity to successfully land an intact rocket back on Earth after a space mission.

SpaceX is an aerospace company that practices astronautics. Those who work in astronautics design, build, and launch rockets, satellites, and other equipment used to travel beyond the earth's atmosphere, to other planets, and even to distant stars. Another, larger sector of the aerospace industry is aviation. Those who work in aviation design, produce, and operate aircraft, helicopters, and drones, or unmanned aerial vehicles (UAVs) for civilian and military use.

Working on the Future

For those who dream of shooting for the stars via rockets, satellites, airplanes, and other high-flying hardware, a career in aviation or aerospace might be their key to the future. People in the aviation and aerospace industries bring their A game to work every day. They rely on their creativity, analytical skills, and knack for science, technology, and math to perform a dizzying array of tasks where accuracy and precision are the only options. When a 450-ton (408-metric-ton) Boeing 747 takes off and lands safely (as hundreds do every day), it is due to the collective skills of aerospace and aviation technicians and mechanics, air traffic controllers, and meteorologists. When the National Aeronautics and Space Administration (NASA) conducts high-tech experiments in the International Space Station (ISS) or guides a robotic rover across the surface of Mars, it is relying on the talents of astronauts, aerospace engineers, and planetary scientists.

While NASA, SpaceX, and Boeing are among the most high-profile organizations involved in aviation and aerospace, nearly half of the industry's revenue comes from the defense contracts with the US government. Companies like General Electric, Raytheon, and Lockheed Martin employ thousands of aerospace workers who design and manufacture jet engines, radar systems, satellites, and defense-related information technology. Many government-backed projects are cutting-edge and highly technical; workers are called on to use extensive problem-solving skills that are rarely required in other fields. Additionally, NASA and the US Department of Defense plan projects with time frames of ten, twenty, and even thirty years. In a December 2012 online aerospace industry review, business publisher WetFeet explains the excitement involved in operating in such a milieu: "The effect for people working in the industry is that you get to work on things that are decades ahead of what the general public will ever see."

Healthy Growth Predicted

Aerospace and aviation employed 1.2 million people in 2015, with another 3.2 million working indirectly for the industry. Aerospace and aviation jobs can be found in nearly every state, but seven states account for nearly half of all employment. The state with the most jobs is California, followed (in descending order) by Washington, Texas, Florida, Arizona, Connecticut, and Kansas. Taken as a whole, the aerospace and aviation sector is one of the top employers in the

Careers in Aviation and Aerospace

Occupation	Entry-Level Education	2015 Median Pay
Aerospace Engineer	Bachelor's degree	$107,830
Aerospace Engineering and Operations Technician	Associate's degree	$66,180
Aircraft and Avionics Equipment Mechanic and Technician	FAA certification	$58,390
Airline and Commercial Pilot	Commercial pilot license, instrument rating, multiengine rating, Airline Transport Pilot certificate	$102,520
Air Traffic Controller	Associate's degree	$122,950
Atmospheric Scientist, Including Meteorologist	Bachelor's degree	$89,820
Cartographer and Photogrammetrist	Bachelor's degree	$61,880
Chemist and Materials Scientist	Bachelor's degree	$72,610
Drafter	Associate's degree	$52,720
Flight Attendant	High school diploma or equivalent	$44,860
Geoscientist	Bachelor's degree	$89,700
Mathematician	Master's degree	$111,110
Physicist and Astronomer	Doctoral or professional degree	$110,980
Technical Writer	Bachelor's degree	$70,240

Source: Bureau of Labor Statistics, *Occupational Outlook Handbook*. www.bls.gov/ooh.

US economy. According to the *US Aerospace & Defense Labor Market Study* by the professional services firm Deloitte, the industry added thirty-nine thousand jobs in 2016, and steady growth is predicted for the coming years. As Deloitte vice chair Tom Captain wrote in the report: "This sector's jobs are also paying almost twice the national average. . . . A return to growth will be healthy for innovation, product development and game-changing technology creation—a cornerstone of this industry."

People have long dreamed about soaring through the sky, flying into outer space, and visiting the planets. In the twenty-first century, thousands of people go to work every day to make those long-held dreams a reality.

Aerospace Engineer

What Does an Aerospace Engineer Do?

Everyone has heard the expression "It doesn't take a rocket scientist" when referring to the accomplishment of some simple task. But some tasks do require the attention of rocket scientists, such as developing, testing, and implementing new technologies like rocket engines, launch vehicles, satellites, spacecraft, weapons, and other equipment that travels above Earth's atmosphere.

Real rocket scientists call themselves aerospace engineers, and since a typical rocket contains over 3 million parts, aerospace engineers work in a number of highly specialized fields. Some engineers design and test structural systems—that is, launch vehicle bodies made up of a rocket nose cone, frame, and fins. Others work on propulsion systems, which include rocket engines, fuel systems, pumps, nozzles, and other equipment. Those who design and test guidance systems are involved with sophisticated sensors, onboard computers, radar,

---

At a Glance:

Aerospace Engineer

Minimum Educational Requirements

Bachelor's degree in aerospace engineering or related science fields

Personal Qualities

Critical-thinking, complex problem-solving, and strong reading skills

Certification and Licensing

None

Working Conditions

Offices, laboratories, or manufacturing environments

Salary Range

As of 2015, $61,000 to $128,000 per year

Number of Jobs

72,500 as of 2015

Future Job Outlook

A 2 percent decline over the next decade

and digital equipment that provides stability and control. Payload engineers spend their days working on equipment that rockets take into orbit, such as satellites, spacecraft, and robots. And these are just the major systems—out of dozens—that an aerospace engineer can focus on. In 2011 aerospace engineer John Connolly of the Johnson Space Center provided an overview of his job for a career guide on the Texas Workforce Commission website:

> My main responsibility is to try to find safe ways for people to travel beyond Earth orbit, to places like the moon and Mars. At the same time that we're designing these missions for people, I'm also thinking about the robots we need to send out to explore the places the people might go. To design missions that might happen 10 or 20 years in the future, we need to predict future advances in technology.

This work requires an aerospace engineer to know numerous complex scientific premises. Aerodynamics focuses on the motion of air and how it interacts with solid objects like launch vehicles. Thermodynamics is the study of how heat and temperature interact with energy and movement in, say, a rocket engine. Authorities on propulsion systems work to create power from a propulsive force such as a rocket engine. Specialists in electrically powered propulsion study laser- and solar-powered systems used to power spacecraft in orbit.

Aerospace engineers often alternate between conducting hard science and dealing with paperwork and bureaucracy. Some manage production, oversee quality control, program computers, or design software. And an aerospace engineer might spend his or her days assessing proposals for projects, determining their feasibility, and drawing up budgets. Those lucky enough to work at NASA often combine numerous skills, as aerospace technologist Julie A. Pollitt told the Career Cornerstone Center in an online interview about her job: "Whereas a lot of people I talk to in big companies, they'll have one specific area. They may do all stress analysis or all fluids analysis or drafting. I mean, they're not [working in] the whole broad range. [At NASA] we're jacks-of-all-trades."

NASA rocket scientists like Pollitt are often the public face of the aerospace industry. But not all aerospace engineers work on spacecraft. Others focus on the design and operation of commercial and military airplanes, helicopters, and remotely piloted aircraft and rotorcraft, or drones.

There is no typical day on the job for an aerospace engineer because of the specialized nature of the industry. An engineer might conduct research on materials used in aircraft production or spend days analyzing an airplane's structural reliability. Those who work in defense may oversee a team designing missile guidance systems or conducting test flights with jet fighter pilots. Research engineers test equipment and theories needed to build futuristic hypersonic vehicles or reusable launch vehicles. Construction engineers spend their days ensuring that designs are properly implemented within a customer's budget and schedule. Elizabeth Bierman, a customer support engineer at Honeywell Aerospace, explained her workdays on the Lifehacker website: "I have been able to travel to the job site (airport hangars) and help our customers install the navigation system into the aircraft. I also have traveled around the world to work with our airline customers to talk with them about how they can use our products better."

In the highly technical world of aeronautical engineering, projects and opportunities are equally diverse. For example, on the NASAPeople website, flight systems engineer Steve Jensen describes his job: "I carry out systems engineering, programming, and experiment integration on the F-18 System Research Aircraft. Right now we've just completed flight test of an electromechanical actuator in place of the hydraulic actuator on the left aileron of the aircraft."

How Do You Become an Aerospace Engineer?

Education

More than 75 percent of aerospace engineers have a bachelor's degree. Those who wish to work in aerospace need to obtain a bachelor of science in mechanical engineering or aerospace engineering. Both fields of study focus on fluid mechanics, thermodynamics, materials science (solid mechanics and metallurgy), and dynamics (controls and machine design). Some students might be interested in classes in space

Aerospace engineers work in any number of highly specialized jobs, including design and testing of structural systems, propulsion systems, and guidance systems. Their work might involve airplanes, jets, helicopters, or spacecraft.

mission design and launch vehicle design, and they might take lab courses in robotics. Those who go on to pursue a master of science in aerospace might attend courses in systems design theory, fluid dynamic flow issues, interaction in spacecraft environments, and rocket fuel propulsion mechanics.

To prepare for such college courses, high school students should focus on STEM subjects: science, technology, engineering, and math. Aerospace engineers make extensive use of physics and chemistry, so candidates for this career should have good grades in these subjects. Computer skills are also very important, and aspiring aerospace engineers should not be afraid to learn as much about computer operation as possible. In an interview with the Aerospaceweb.org website, aerospace engineer Joe Yoon explains: "I only had to learn one computer language through my coursework, but I found it useful to take classes in two others on the side, and the more you know, the more popular you'll be during the job hunt!" Beyond technical skills, aerospace work relies on teamwork, so communication classes like speech and writing will help individuals express their ideas more effectively.

Certification and Licensing

Aerospace engineers who work at big companies or for the government are not required to have a special license. However, those who are self-employed or work for small businesses need to become a professional engineer (PE). This requires the engineer to pass a Fundamentals of Engineering exam, work under a licensed PE for four years, and then take a Principles and Practice of Engineering exam. (The work requirement is difficult to fulfill because there are so few PEs to work under in the aerospace field.)

Many aerospace companies have contracts with the US Department of Defense. An engineer who works on classified or military programs is required to have a security clearance, which takes six months to a year to obtain, after being hired. The clearance may be listed at one of the following levels: confidential, secret, or top secret. Those who wish to obtain a security clearance need to answer a number of very personal questions about themselves and their spouse, children, parents, and siblings. They need to provide numerous details about everywhere they have ever lived, worked, and traveled outside the United States. They will be asked about their police record, use of illegal drugs, financial history, and mental health problems.

Volunteer Work and Internships

High school students interested in aerospace should consider applying for an internship position. NASA offers research internships at various facilities throughout the country to students with good grades who are at least sixteen years old. Northrop Grumman, Hawker Pacific Aerospace, and other private companies also take on a limited number of summer interns. College sophomores can apply for cooperative education programs (co-ops). Students in co-ops stop taking classes in order to work full time. The positions are typically paid and last anywhere from three to twelve months. Students receive an academic credit and letter grade for their paid work experience.

Co-ops and internships provide an opportunity to work in a professional environment, get good references, and develop a network of like-minded professionals. All this will give students a competitive advantage when job hunting. Engineer Trevor Jones participated in a co-op program at NASA before landing an engineering position at the space agency. As Jones said in an interview with the Career Zoo: "When you're in college definitely take advantage of the internship or co-op programs that they might have. . . . It might be the most important thing you're going to get out of college, that real-world experience and an opportunity to get a job when you graduate."

Skills and Personality

Becoming an aerospace engineer requires long hours of study of the most complex subjects imaginable. Successful engineers have ambition, analytical and scientific skills, and a passion for aircraft, spacecraft, and flight technology. Aerospace engineers need to have excellent communication skills, technical knowledge, and the ability to plan and manage projects effectively and within budget. In this ever-changing field, aerospace engineers are committed to staying up-to-date on the latest developments in the field.

On the Job

Employers

Most aerospace engineers work for firms that design and manufacture aircraft and aircraft components, such as Bell Helicopter, Northrop Grumman, Lockheed Martin, and Boeing. Those who design and manufacture spacecraft and spacecraft components work for government agencies such as NASA and the Defense Department.

Working Conditions

Aerospace engineers may work indoors in offices, laboratories, classrooms, or factories, or outdoors in test areas. They often work closely in teams with other engineers and support personnel. They put in regular forty-hour weeks, but overtime, including weekends and holidays, may be required. The job can be mentally exhausting, and work conditions can be stressful when project deadlines loom.

Earnings

Average starting salaries for an aeronautical engineer are around $61,000 a year. Those who have been on the job for five to ten years can expect to earn around $85,000, while highly experienced aerospace engineers can bring in $128,000 annually.

Opportunities for Advancement

When compared with other engineering fields, aerospace engineers have great potential for advancement. Some who begin work as a member of a research or design team may be promoted to larger, more complex projects. Aerospace companies often pay for further training, which can lead to a promotion to a supervisory post. Advancement can also take place outside of company structures. For example, an engineering career might begin with an entry-level job at an aerospace firm. After five or ten years, the engineer might get a job with NASA or become a professor or researcher at a university.

What Is the Future Outlook for Aerospace Engineers?

According to the Bureau of Labor Statistics (BLS), opportunities in aerospace engineering are expected to shrink by 2 percent between 2016 and 2024 because most engineers are employed in manufacturing industries that are not expected to see much growth in the next decade. However, the BLS also notes that job prospects are expected to grow by 5 percent for aerospace engineers who specialize in research and development, engine design, and production.

Find Out More

American Institute for Aeronautics and Astronautics (AIAA)
12700 Sunrise Valley Dr., Suite 200
Reston, VA 20191-5807
website: www.aiaa.org

The AIAA is the world's largest aerospace publisher and acts as a voice and information resource for aerospace engineers, scientists, policy makers, students, and educators.

American Physical Society (APS)
1 Physics Ellipse
College Park, MD 20740-3844
website: www.aps.org

The APS is an organization of physicists who work in the aerospace field and elsewhere to advance science, science education, and the science community. The organization supports physics educators and students at all levels through its programs, publications, and resources.

Engineers Without Borders
1031 33rd St., Suite 210
Denver, CO 80205
website: www.ewb-usa.org

Engineers Without Borders is dedicated to improving the lives of people through engineering projects—such as building solar energy capabilities or clean water installations—that allow communities to meet their basic human needs. The group, whose members come from many fields, including aerospace, offers educational opportunities to those interested in managing engineering projects domestically and internationally.

Society of Women Engineers (SWE)
203 N. La Salle St., Suite 1675
Chicago, IL 60601
website: http://societyofwomenengineers.swe.org

The SWE is dedicated to giving women engineers a unique voice within the aerospace and engineering industries. The organization runs a K–12 outreach program, provides scholarships to female students, and sponsors individual and collegiate competition awards competitions.

Aerospace Engineering and Operations Technician

At a Glance:

Aerospace Engineering and Operations Technician

Minimum Educational Requirements
Associate's degree

Personal Qualities
Communication and critical-thinking skills; computer, math, and mechanical abilities; detail oriented

Certification and Licensing
An Airmen Certification issued by the Federal Aviation Administration is preferred by employers but not required

Working Conditions
Indoors in labs, offices, and manufacturing sites; outdoors on runways and launch sites

Salary Range
As of 2015, $39,560 to $99,090 per year

Number of Jobs
11,400 in 2015

Future Job Outlook
Number of jobs expected to increase 4 percent by 2024

What Does an Aerospace Engineering and Operations Technician Do?

Aerospace engineering and operations technicians have a long job title that comes with a lot of responsibilities. People who work as aerospace engineering and operations techs test aircraft systems, maintain complex flight equipment, carry out the designs of aerospace engineers, and even turn nuts and bolts on rocket engines. Although most did not study challenging college courses like thermodynamics and physics, they work alongside researchers, scientists, engineers, pilots, and astronauts in the aerospace business.

Aerospace engineering and operations technicians, sometimes referred to simply as operations technicians, play an important role in the aerospace industry. They work closely with aerospace engineers to build, test, and maintain vehicles for air and space travel that the engineers design. In doing so, aerospace engineering and operations technicians perform many tasks. They operate and calibrate computer systems to ensure tests are accurate. They fabricate parts from aluminum, steel, and brass using lathes, drill presses, welders, grinders, and polishers. And they oversee installation of parts, instruments, and systems in airplanes, helicopters, and spacecraft. Aerospace engineering and operations technicians operate wind tunnels, conduct trials in laboratories, build test equipment, create models of aircraft and spacecraft, and support many types of research. In videos where dozens of NASA workers in a control room cheer after some critical maneuver is achieved in outer space, a few of those people are aerospace engineering and operations technicians, who were running tests and watching for errors as the mission went forward.

There is little room for error in this field, and engineering and operations technicians must perform their duties with absolute precision. A tech might run a million-dollar computer numerical control machine that cuts metal aircraft parts so precisely that they are within a thousandth of an inch of the designer's specifications.

The work done by aerospace engineering and operations techs was in the news in January 2016 when the US military tested an antimissile interceptor. The interceptor is designed to hit a rocket launched from a hostile nation such as North Korea or Iran. The operation, which is compared to hitting a bullet with another bullet, depended on a part called a divert thruster, which helps steer the interceptor toward the enemy missile. The army conducted a test, which cost $250 million, to make sure the divert thruster worked with the interceptor. The test involved hundreds of aerospace engineering and operations techs, who were stationed at various military installations and on ships in the Pacific Ocean. However, the test was a failure; the interceptor did not hit the dummy incoming missile during the test. This left aerospace engineering and operations techs at the army's Redstone Arsenal in

Huntsville, Alabama, to analyze data from the test flight to determine what went wrong.

Job titles for aerospace engineering and operations technicians can be as varied as the equipment they work on. Systems mechanics assemble, install, and maintain major aircraft systems such as flight controls, landing gear, and hydraulics. Structures mechanics fabricate and install aircraft body parts like the fuselage, wings, and stabilizers. Propulsion test technicians analyze and install instruments and electrical systems on jets or rockets.

Most aerospace engineering and operations techs work forty-hour weeks but are often called on to work overtime to meet deadlines. But the specific workday of an operations tech can vary greatly because of the specialized nature of the industry. The work performed by the forty-five aerospace engineering and operations technicians at Rotorcraft Support Inc. (RSI) in Van Nuys, California, provides an example of a typical workday. RSI maintains helicopters for many organizations, including the Pacific tuna fishing fleet, law enforcement agencies, and public utilities. A tech at RSI might provide routine maintenance in the morning and repair rotor heads or overhaul a transmission in the afternoon. In a 2016 profile on the Vertical website, RSI chief executive officer Phil DiFiore says, "We strive to employ positive, experienced, and motivated people that have a passion for the helicopter industry and want to continue to learn."

How Do You Become an Aerospace Engineering and Operations Technician?

Education

High school students interested in becoming aerospace engineering and operations technicians should focus on math, science, drafting, and computer classes. Operations techs work with tools and machinery, so students might want to take extracurricular courses in auto repair or metal fabrication when possible.

Aerospace engineering and operations technicians work in what is known as advanced manufacturing. Economists call their jobs middle-skill work; they require more training than high school but less than a bachelor's degree. That translates into attaining a two-year associate's degree in engineering technology or aerospace technology. Associate's degrees in these subjects can be obtained at community colleges, technical schools, and extension divisions of colleges and universities.

Certification and Licensing

Aerospace engineering and operations technicians do not require special licenses. However, the Federal Aviation Administration (FAA) offers what it calls Airmen Certification to flight engineers, technicians, mechanics, pilots, dispatchers, and navigators. To obtain this certification, applicants are required to pass various tests concerning aviation, FAA regulations, and safety procedures. Employers prefer operations techs who have an Airmen Certification because it provides proof that the technician can understand and carry out the instructions and plans of aerospace engineers.

Most aerospace companies and government agencies design equipment for national defense programs. This means an operations tech must pass an extensive background check to obtain a security clearance. Journalist Elvis Michael describes the process on the Chron website: "Background checks typically include local, state and federal crime records, driving records and credit scores. Some employers require top-level security clearance. Not having a clean record will limit job opportunities in industries that hire the most aerospace engineering technicians."

Volunteer Work and Internships

Many colleges participate in work-study programs in conjunction with aerospace employers. These programs allow students to gain valuable firsthand experience while working to attain an associate's degree in aerospace technology.

Skills and Personality

Mechanical skills and an aptitude for math are the two qualities most important to an aerospace engineering and operations technician.

Math is used every day to make and record precise measurements, operate high-tech equipment, and analyze problems. Mechanical skills come into play when operations techs remove or install parts and fix equipment. Communication skills are also valued because operations techs must be able to understand directions and communicate problems with engineers and team leaders. Critical-thinking abilities are needed to evaluate systems, troubleshoot glitches, and find answers to problems. Operations techs also need to stay on top of changes in the industry and advancements in technology, which introduce new methods and procedures.

On the Job

Employers

Aerospace engineering and operations techs work for aircraft maintenance companies, airlines, government agencies like NASA and the Department of Defense, and private space transportation companies like SpaceX. They also work for aerospace product and parts manufacturing companies like Boeing and defense industry organizations such as Lockheed Martin. Universities and research institutions also hire a limited number of aerospace engineering and operations technicians to teach.

Working Conditions

Aerospace engineering and operations technicians do not spend their days sitting at their desks staring at computer monitors. They often spend their time hustling between laboratories, manufacturing floors, aircraft hangars, and runways or launch sites. Aerospace engineering and operations techs operate heavy machinery and clamber all over aircraft, helicopters, or spacecraft. Sometimes they work in cramped places like the underside of an instrument panel in a jet airliner. The work involves handling tools and sometimes hoisting heavy equipment. Production lines and test centers can be noisy, and workers are required to wear ear protection. But people who work in this field are the unsung heroes of the aerospace industry. Their efforts ensure the safety and well-being of everyone from airline passengers to astronauts on the International Space Station.

Earnings

According to the Bureau of Labor Statistics (BLS), the median annual pay for an aerospace engineering and operations technician in 2015 was $66,180. The lowest-paid aerospace engineering and operations technicians earned $39,560, while workers in the top 10 percent earned $99,090 per year. The highest-paid workers were involved in the research and development segment of the industry, while the lowest-paid worked for testing laboratories.

Opportunities for Advancement

Aerospace engineering and operations technicians starting their careers work under the supervision of more experienced technicians, engineers, and scientists. Those who gain experience will be given more difficult assignments with less supervision. As workers gain experience, they can eventually become supervisors.

What Is the Future Outlook for Aerospace Engineering and Operations Technicians?

The BLS says that about 11,400 people work as aerospace engineering and operations technicians. The agency predicts that employment in the field will grow 4 percent by 2024—slightly slower than the average of 7 percent for all occupations. Fortunately, there is little chance that these jobs will be outsourced to other countries because of the classified nature of the work. Additionally, the airline industry is in the process of redesigning and upgrading much of its equipment to make it more environmentally friendly—quieter and more fuel efficient. This is expected to raise demand for those who work as operations techs in airline research and development.

There is another factor at work for those who can perform skilled tech jobs; at companies like Boeing in Huntington Beach, California, a large percentage of the workforce consists of aging baby boomers who are ready to retire. As the facility's senior manager, Barbara

Mason, told the *Orange County Register* in August 2016, "There are a large number of people with white and gray hair." And the problem is not unique to Boeing. According to a study by the Boston Consulting Group, the average age of skilled manufacturing workers in 2016 was fifty-six. This means Boeing and other aerospace companies need a young workforce to remain competitive. As Mason said in the *Orange County Register*, "When we go to recruit, we are concerned about the [jobs] pipeline. Our contracts are often for five years, and we're looking at retirements. Can we fill these jobs with [young workers who have] technical skills and program-management skills?"

Another growth area for aerospace engineering and operations techs will be in the unmanned aerial vehicle (UAV), or drone, industry. Drones are expected to take a much larger role in industry, entertainment, and defense. Research and development projects, such as designing more efficient propulsion systems and improving UAV flight capabilities, will create demand for aerospace engineering and operations technicians.

Find Out More

Accreditation Board for Engineering and Technology (ABET)
415 N. Charles St.
Baltimore, MD 21201
website: www.abet.org

ABET accredits college and university programs in applied science, computing, engineering, and engineering technology at the associate's, bachelor's, and master's degree levels. ABET accreditation provides assurance that a college or university program meets the quality standards of the profession for which that program prepares graduates. The organization's website provides lists of ABET-accredited programs, information about attaining accreditation, and links to information about workshops and scholarships.

American Institute for Aeronautics and Astronautics (AIAA)
12700 Sunrise Valley Dr., Suite 200
Reston, VA 20191-5807
website: www.aiaa.org

The AIAA is the world's largest aerospace publisher and the principal voice and information resource for aerospace engineer and operating technicians, students, and educators. The AIAA offers a wide range of learning and employment opportunities to those in the aerospace field.

American Society for Engineering Education (ASEE)
1818 N St. NW, Suite 600
Washington DC 20036
website: www.asee.org

The ASEE works with corporations, government agencies, and educational institutions to promote activities that support increased student enrollments in engineering and engineering technology colleges and universities. The organization's website offers publications, blogs, and videos and promotes fellowships for high school students, undergraduates, and graduates.

Women in Aviation International (WAI)
3647 State Route 503 S.
West Alexandria, OH 45381-9354
website: www.wai.org

WAI is dedicated to the encouragement and advancement of women in aviation careers, including aerospace workers, astronauts, corporate pilots, maintenance technicians, and air traffic controllers. WAI offers educational outreach programs and scholarships and sponsors the Girls in Aviation Day program for girls ages eight to seventeen.

Aircraft and Avionics Equipment Mechanic

At a Glance:

Aircraft and Avionics Equipment Mechanic

Minimum Educational Requirements

Certificate of completion from a federally approved aviation maintenance technical school

Personal Qualities

Self-motivated, hardworking, mechanical aptitude, good communication skills

Certification and Licensing

Certification by the Federal Aviation Administration

Working Conditions

Indoors in airplane hangars or outdoors alongside runways and passenger terminals

Salary Range

The median pay for aircraft mechanics is $55,210 per year; for avionics technicians, $58,540

Number of Jobs

About 137,300 jobs in 2015

Future Job Outlook

Little or no change before 2025

What Does an Aircraft and Avionics Equipment Mechanic Do?

While people might not want to think about it while jetting across the continent, airplanes need constant maintenance to avoid breaking down as the miles fly by. That is why the work of aviation and avionics equipment mechanics is so important. They make sure that everything from piston-driven propeller planes to diesel helicopters to $350 million Boeing 747 commercial jets are protected from mechanical failure.

Aircraft and avionics equipment mechanics are skilled technicians who keep various types of airplanes and helicopters operating efficiently and safely. They service, repair, and overhaul vital components, including airframes, engines, propellers, hydraulic systems, and aircraft instruments. Aircraft and avionics equipment mechanics employed by airlines perform routine maintenance, repairs, and inspections on jets and other aircraft that are in-service, or in regular use. These workers might also perform major overhauls or upgrades to meet updated regulations from the Federal Aviation Administration (FAA), which oversees all aspects of American civil aviation.

Other aircraft and avionics equipment mechanics are employed in what is called general aviation. These mechanics often work on smaller propeller aircraft with piston engines or turbo engines (turboprops). These types of aircraft are often owned by businesses, transportation companies, and hobby pilots. Helicopter mechanics generally perform the same duties as airplane mechanics but sometimes work longer hours, as helicopters require much more maintenance than fixed-wing aircraft.

Those who work in general aviation often have opportunities to travel because their services are in demand. Leo Moroni has been an airplane mechanic in Texas for twenty years, and he still loves his job. "I'll travel throughout Georgia, Florida, I'll fly to the Caribbean, and all of South America to wherever [the airplanes] are and I'll fix them right there," Moroni said in a 2015 career spotlight video for *Flying* magazine. "I've never had a day that I actually did not feel like coming to work."

Those with a special interest in electronics might choose to specialize in avionics. Techs in this field work on equipment and systems that control flight, engine functions, and other important facets, including navigation, communications radios, weather radar systems, autopilots, and computer systems. Avionics techs work side by side with aircraft mechanics, and many are cross-trained; they can work on power plants, airframes, and other aircraft systems.

Most aircraft and avionics equipment mechanics specialize. Job titles include airframe and power plant mechanic, avionics technician, inspection authorized (IA) mechanic, and designated airworthiness representative (DAR). Some of these are installation and repair positions, and others are testing and supervisory posts.

A&P mechanics are certified to perform many maintenance and alteration jobs on aircraft engines, landing gear, breaks, and air-conditioning systems. These mechanics perform work according to FAA regulations. Maintenance schedules are based on several factors, including number of hours an aircraft has been flown, the number of trips taken, or the number of days since the last inspection. Mechanics measure wear and identify corrosion and microscopic defects in the airframe, wings, and tail with precision tools such as X-ray machines, magnetic scanners, and ultrasonic scanners.

As with modern automobiles, power plant problems are diagnosed from digital information provided by sensors on the aircraft's various systems. When problems are found, A&P mechanics make repairs on the problem areas. After repairs are finished and the equipment is tested, mechanics create detailed records about the problems found and the work completed.

Avionics technicians are specialists; some work inside aircraft, while others are bench technicians and system troubleshooters. Those who work in general avionics test and maintain electronic equipment on fixed-wing aircraft and helicopters. If a problem is found, the technician removes the device and sends it to a shop, where a bench technician will fix it.

Avionics bench techs are hands-on specialists who work on dozens of different electronic aircraft components, from communications radios to large radar antennas. Many of the circuit boards techs deal with contain hundreds of tiny connections. Bench techs need good eyesight and steady hands, as they peer through binocular magnifiers or microscopes wielding small hand tools and soldering irons to repair delicate wires and circuits.

System troubleshooters are generally avionics techs who have years of experience. They have a deep understanding of aircraft and aviation systems and the ways the systems function and interact with one another. System troubleshooters supervise aviation and bench techs and are consulted to diagnose difficult problems.

IA mechanics are among the highest-ranking personnel in the aircraft repair and maintenance business. Workers certified by the FAA with an IA designation are also certified A&P mechanics. IAs inspect and test aircraft after major repairs or alterations are completed. They ensure that replacement parts conform to approved standards and that the repaired aircraft is equal to its original condition. According to the FAA's *Inspection Authorization Information Guide*, "The holder of an IA must personally perform the inspection. The regulations do not provide for delegation of this responsibility. Approving major repairs and major alterations is a serious responsibility. The approval action should consist of a detailed investigation."

Once the IA signs off on an aircraft, the designated airworthiness representative takes over. DARs focus on the airworthiness of an aircraft. Their work involves examining, inspecting, and testing aircraft. DARs issue airworthiness certificates required by the FAA before the aircraft can leave the ground.

How Do You Become an Aircraft and Avionics Equipment Mechanic?

Education

Most aircraft and avionics equipment mechanics learn their trade in the military or at FAA-approved aviation maintenance technician schools. Students who plan to attend an aviation maintenance tech school will find high school coursework like electronics, computers, and auto shop helpful. While cars are mechanically different from airplanes, working on them will help students understand how engines and systems work and help them get used to handling tools and test equipment. Students will also need to build good communication skills. The FAA requires aircraft mechanics to read and understand complex regulations and submit detailed reports about repairs and maintenance to the agency.

Students who want to become aircraft and avionics equipment mechanics will be required to follow numerous rules and regulations laid out in trade jargon. This refers to phrases, acronyms, and abbreviations that would baffle most people. It starts with the schooling; the FAA refers to an aviation maintenance technical school as an AMTS. These schools are required to train students to meet the provisions of Title 14, Part 147 of the Code of Federal Regulations (14 CFR). This means students will be attending an FAA-approved, Part 147 AMTS. These schools provide a certificate of completion that allows students to take FAA exams relevant to their field.

Aircraft and avionics equipment mechanics are skilled technicians who keep all types of aircraft operating efficiently and safely. They service, repair, and overhaul vital components, including airframes, engines, propellers, hydraulic systems, and aircraft instruments.

There are about 170 Part 147 AMTSs in the United States. By law, students who graduate from one of these schools must have completed nineteen hundred class hours. This generally takes place over the course of two years. Depending on their major (aviation technology, avionics, or aviation maintenance), students complete courses in math, physics, chemistry, computer science, and mechanical drawing. They study the latest technology used in turbine engines, composite airframe materials, and aviation electronics. Upon graduation, students need to be certified by the FAA. And that is just the beginning of the journey. As Moroni said in his *Flying* video interview, "The training that you get when you first go to school, that's critical in itself. Without it you won't pass [the FAA] exam. The greater thing is, it actually doesn't stop there because once you get that license, that's only a license to learn. Continuously trying to learn more is what makes you understand every system in an airplane and that's what makes you a great troubleshooter."

Certification and Licensing

While some aircraft and avionics equipment mechanics do not have licenses or certification, they receive less pay than certified workers. Additionally, those without credentials can only work under the supervision of certified mechanics. Most obtain certification because it improves their chances to find employment and receive higher wages. The FAA offers two types of certification: An airframe mechanic, or A, is certified for bodywork, while a power plant mechanic, or P, works on engines. Most employers prefer those who have both certifications, or A&P mechanics. To obtain certification, mechanics must be at least eighteen years old and US citizens who can read, write, and speak English. An applicant must have at least eighteen months' work experience to qualify for either an A or a P, or thirty months to qualify for an A&P. However, the successful completion of courses at a Part 147 AMTS serves as a substitute for the work requirements. To obtain certification, applicants must pass a number of oral, written, and practical exams within a two-year period.

Avionics techs usually possess an airframe certification but can obtain other types of credentials. The National Center for Aerospace & Transportation Technologies issues an aircraft electronics technician certification that certifies avionics techs have a basic level of knowledge in specific subject areas related to their jobs. Avionics techs who work on communications equipment might need a radio-telephone operator certification issued by the Federal Communications Commission.

Skills and Personality

Every day thousands of fliers put their lives in the hands of aircraft and avionics equipment mechanics. This is not a job for people with sloppy work habits or the inability to work efficiently under pressure. Employers are seeking those who are self-motivated and hardworking and who exhibit a high degree of mechanical aptitude. Aviation and avionics workers must multitask as they diagnose and solve complex problems while keeping detailed records of their work. As technology advances, the complex machinery on aircraft is becoming even more complicated, and workers need to stay current and update their skills to deal with the latest changes.

On the Job

Employers

Aircraft and avionics equipment mechanics perform routine maintenance for major airlines at airports throughout the United States. Major overhauls of commercial jets are conducted at airline facilities in New York, Los Angeles, Miami, Minneapolis, Denver, Atlanta, Tulsa, and Kansas City. Thousands of A&P mechanics work in general aviation at air taxi services, flight training schools, aerial spraying companies, corporate jet facilities, and other private enterprises. The US government employs civilian aircraft and avionics mechanics to work on military aircraft and at the FAA overhaul facility in Oklahoma City.

Working Conditions

Aircraft and avionics equipment mechanics work in hangars and on runways for major airlines, private air transport companies, aircraft maintenance businesses, and government agencies like police and fire departments. Much of the work is done at night. Most commercial pilots fly aircraft during the day and write up problems in a log book. Mechanics and tech workers try to solve these problems before the aircraft is needed in the morning.

Earnings

According to the Bureau of Labor Statistics (BLS), the median annual wage for aircraft mechanics in 2014 was $55,210, with the most experienced workers earning around $76,660. Avionics technicians earned an average of $58,540 per year.

Opportunities for Advancement

Aircraft mechanics who gain experience might advance to a career as a lead mechanic, lead inspector, or shop supervisor. Aircraft or avionics mechanics and technicians may also obtain work as an FAA inspector or open their own aircraft maintenance and repair shop.

What Is the Future Outlook for Aircraft and Avionics Equipment Mechanics?

According to the BLS, the number of people working as aircraft and avionics equipment mechanics is expected to grow by less than 1 percent by 2024, which means there will be little change in the number of jobs available.

Find Out More

Aircraft Electronics Association (AEA)
3570 NE Ralph Powell Rd.
Lee's Summit, MO 64064
website: www.aea.net

The AEA represents numerous government-certified repair facilities and equipment manufacturers, along with avionics engineers and educational institutions. The association offers training courses, scholarships, and publications of interest to students and avionics workers.

AMT Society
1233 Janesville Ave.
Fort Atkinson, WI 53538
website: www.amtsociety.org

The website of the AMT (Aircraft Maintenance Technology) Society has numerous educational resources, including information about becoming an aircraft mechanic, finding a school, and FAA testing and certification.

Aviation Institute of Maintenance (AIM)
4455 South Blvd.
Virginia Beach, VA 23452
website: www.aviationmaintenance.edu

The AIM is an educational institution with eleven campuses that teach Part 147 FAA-approved courses. The website describes details concerning numerous courses that allow students to pursue careers as avionics techs, aviation maintenance technicians, helicopter mechanics, and more.

Commercial Pilot

When commercial airline pilots stride through airports in their crisp uniforms, they command respect. Perhaps this is what inspired Chris Manno to announce to his parents when he was three years old that that he wanted to be a pilot. While thousands of kids make similar declarations every day, Manno followed his dream. Today he is a captain for American Airlines who has spent the past thirty-five years flying commercial jets. In a 2015 interview on the Lifehacker website, Manno called his job "pushing the metal" across the sky.

While commercial pilots are often associated with "pushing the metal," most of their work takes place on the ground. They plan routes, prepare for flights, and consult with ground crews and other aviation personnel. Pilots also spend a great deal of time preparing for and taking tests. They are required to regularly see doctors for physical exams and take biannual tests to remain in compliance with Federal

At a Glance:
Commercial Pilot

Minimum Educational Requirements
High school diploma, 1,000 hours of flight training

Personal Qualities
Communication skills, quick reaction time, observational abilities, problem-solving skills

Certification and Licensing
Commercial pilot license, instrument rating, multiengine rating, airline transport pilot certificate

Working Conditions
In aircraft; sometimes spend days away from home because of overnight layovers

Salary Range
$25,000 to $200,000 per year

Number of Jobs
119,000 in May 2015

Future Job Outlook
A 5 percent growth by 2024

Aviation Administration (FAA) regulations. The pilots' rigorous routine helps make air travel the safest mode of transportation by far. But it also means that airline pilots often work twelve or more hours a day while spending only a few hours at the controls of an aircraft.

Commercial pilots fly small propeller airplanes, helicopters, corporate aircraft, cargo planes, passenger jets, air ambulances, and sightseeing planes. Their work involves the meticulous planning of each flight before leaving the ground. Pilots spend many hours checking the weather and confirming flight plans before departure. They perform preflight equipment checks and fill out flight logs. When planning a route, they must consider performance issues such as the aircraft's weight, power, and speed. After takeoff, pilots must flawlessly execute dozens of complex navigation and operation procedures.

Most of what airline pilots do takes place behind closed doors, either in the restricted flight operations area of the airport or inside a locked cockpit. On the ground there are constant inspections, drug tests, and checking and rechecking of equipment and procedures. In the air pilots are aided by autopilot and computers, but this equipment cannot replace a human operator. Pilots must be skilled in maneuvers like taking off, climbing, descending, and landing while simultaneously dealing with weather conditions, fuel management, and avoidance of other aircraft. "My job includes having backup plans to backup plans as far as fuel, duration, route, and even destination goes," Manno told Lifehacker. "I stay three steps ahead of the aircraft and flight at all times. . . . With weather, short runways, crowded airspace, and complex approaches . . . there's a lot to handle." Fortunately, passenger jet pilots do not have to go it alone; they work with copilots, called first officers, who share flight duties such as communicating with air traffic controllers and monitoring engines and other aircraft systems during flight.

How Do You Become a Commercial Pilot?

Education

Becoming a licensed commercial pilot takes time and money. Most airlines only hire pilots with a bachelor's degree (in any subject). In addition, those who wish to become commercial pilots must take flight training from certified instructors or at flight schools. Pilot training is offered by some colleges and universities as part of two- and four-year aviation degree programs. Flight instruction can cost around $100 an hour, and experts say a student can take on $150,000 in debt to obtain a commercial pilot rating—that is about the same amount of debt accumulated by a medical student.

Certification and Licensing

Anyone wishing to obtain a commercial pilot license from the FAA must accumulate 1,000 hours of flight time. Helicopter training requires another 150 hours of flight time. Additionally, most commercial pilots need an instrument rating—a measure of how well they understand and can navigate by instruments—that allows them to fly through clouds, storms, and other conditions that limit visibility. An instrument rating is also required to carry paying passengers more than 50 miles (80 km) or at night. Commercial pilots are required to pass the FAA practical test, informally called a checkride, two times a year. During this exam, pilots fly in an aircraft with an authorized examiner to demonstrate their skills and competency. Pilots can lose their jobs if they do not pass the checkride.

Commercial airline pilots are required to have an airline transport pilot certificate. This certificate expands various privileges granted by the commercial pilot license. Most who work for large passenger airline companies also receive what is called an aircraft-type rating for each type of jet they fly. For example, an individual might earn an aircraft-type rating for a DC-10, an MD-80, or a Boeing 737-800.

Skills and Personality

As anyone who has seen the cockpit of an aircraft understands, pilots need strong observational skills to keep watch over the dizzying number of screens, gauges, dials, and other instruments that provide critical information about the aircraft's operating systems. Pilots also need good communication skills to clearly convey information to air traffic controllers and crew members, and they must also understand instructions. Pilots need to be problem solvers so they can quickly find solutions to complex issues such as bad weather, turbulence, and equipment failure. And pilots must have quick reaction times to properly respond to any situation that might arise while ferrying 160 passengers across the sky at 600 miles per hour (966 kph).

A pilot needs to be in top physical condition because people's lives depend on the pilot's abilities to stay calm under pressure. Captains must pass a thorough physical exam every six months; other commercial pilots must pass an annual exam. Health problems such as heart disease, high blood pressure, or failing eyesight might end a pilot's career. Additionally, a pilot's job depends on passing regular drug and alcohol tests. The FAA also scrutinizes a pilot's driving and criminal records, and pilots can be fired if they have committed any felonies or have been convicted for driving while intoxicated.

On the Job

Employers

Commercial pilots work wherever airplanes and helicopters take to the air. About fifty thousand pilots are members of the Air Line Pilots Association, a union that represents passenger jet pilots in the United States and Canada. These men and women fly large aircraft made by Boeing, Airbus, and McDonnell Douglas for major airlines such as American, Delta, and United. About seventy thousand other commercial pilots work at jobs in general aviation (GA). GA includes all civilians flying outside scheduled passenger airlines. About 65 percent of those involved in GA are commercial pilots who fly for businesses and public services. Commercial pilots work in businesses that specialize in package delivery, agricultural services (crop dusters who spray crops with chemicals), and even hot-air balloon sightseeing tours. Some commercial pilots fly helicopters for law enforcement agencies, emergency medical services, news and traffic organizations, pipeline and utility inspection companies, and passenger transport firms. The remaining 35 percent of GA pilots are individuals who use their airplanes like the family car for transportation involving travel and work.

Commercial pilots fly all sorts of aircraft—small propeller airplanes, helicopters, corporate aircraft, cargo planes, passenger jets, air ambulances, and sightseeing planes. In addition to flying, they are responsible for checking weather, doing preflight equipment checks, and more.

Working Conditions

Almost every pilot will say that flying an aircraft is the most fun a person can have at work. As an airline pilot known only as Mike put it in a 2014 interview on the Flight Club website: "From the time the cockpit door closes to the time it opens, this is the best job in the world. Flying is the perfect mixture of art, science, and magic. It can also be quite a challenge, but that tends to be when it is most rewarding." Mike also said that there are bad parts to the job. By law, airline pilots cannot fly more than one hundred hours a month, or one thousand hours a year. This means pilots often have variable work schedules, with a few days on and a few days off. Most pilots spend a considerable amount of time away from home and family and often complain about lonely nights in hotel rooms. On the job, pilots endure the same tedium at airports as passengers do. They must deal with security screening, overpriced food in airport terminals, and long delays caused by weather and other problems. Only the largest airports have crew lounges, but even these can be cramped, noisy, and uncomfortable. And just like everyone else, pilots can suffer from jet lag, fatigue caused by flying through different time zones. On Lifehacker, Manno adds his perspective concerning the worst parts of the job: "Definitely the constant scrutiny, testing, evaluations, and requalifications that recur over and over through an airline pilot's career. . . . From Day One as a pilot, you work your butt off."

Life is not much easier for those who work in GA. These pilots often have very irregular schedules; for example, flying thirty hours one month and ninety the next. Because they have so much downtime, GA pilots often have work responsibilities not related to flying, such as helping in the office, performing light maintenance in hangars, and so on. Pilots who fly crop dusters may be exposed to toxic chemicals. Helicopter pilots involved in rescue and police work often fly in dangerous conditions and are subject to personal injury. However, most GA pilots do not spend as many nights away from home, the exception being high-priced business pilots who ferry executives around the globe.

Earnings

Many airline pilots begin their career as copilots at small regional airlines, a job that is neither glamorous nor enriching. First-year copilots can expect to make about $25,000 annually, which is less than a truck driver makes. However, a pilot working for a charter airline can earn around $90,000 per year, while a captain for a major passenger airline or cargo carrier might bring in $110,000. The most experienced pilots can earn up to $200,000 each year.

Corporate pilots with five to nine years of flight service earn between $53,607 and $79,623 annually. The salaries of helicopter pilots range from $81,000 to $150,000 each year, which makes the median annual wage around $111,680. Crop duster pilots earn less, with salaries ranging from $60,000 to $100,000 a year. However, those who own airplanes and spraying businesses can earn much more.

Opportunities for Advancement

Most students who put in the minimum time requirements to obtain a commercial pilot license can usually only find work as flight instructors or as pilots for smaller, charter airlines. After gaining another one thousand hours in the air, a pilot can find work at a regional airline. After attaining four thousand hours of flying time, a pilot can apply for work as a first officer at a major airline, where advancement is determined by union rules. In general, it can take anywhere from five to fifteen years for a copilot to advance to a captain position.

What Is the Future Outlook for Commercial Pilots?

The Bureau of Labor Statistics (BLS) predicts that the number of commercial pilots will grow by about 5 percent by 2024. This means about 5,400 new pilot jobs will be added by this date, or around 600 a year. But the BLS number is conservative compared to a 2015 report by aircraft maker Boeing, which predicted that 95,000 new commercial airline pilots will be needed in the United States during the next twenty years; that is about 4,750 pilots each year. According to Boeing, demand will be even greater in the Asia-Pacific region, where 226,000 new pilots will be needed by 2035.

Find Out More

Aircraft Owners and Pilots Association (AOPA)
421 Aviation Way
Frederick, MD 21701
website: www.aopa.org

The AOPA is dedicated to general aviation, and its website provides comprehensive information about flight schools, safety, and careers in aviation. The Students section provides detailed steps for obtaining a pilot license, with information about scholarships, flight training loans, and purchasing an aircraft.

Air Line Pilots Association (ALPA)
1625 Massachusetts Ave. NW
Washington, DC 20036
website: www.alpa.org

The ALPA represents fifty-three thousand pilots in North America and focuses on safety and security issues. The website provides insight into a commercial pilot's work life, and the association offers four-year undergraduate scholarships to qualified applicants.

International Society of Women Airline Pilots
723 S. Casino Center Blvd., 2nd Floor
Las Vegas, NV 89101-6716
website: www.iswap.org

The International Society of Women Airline Pilots exists to support women who hold commercial pilot licenses. The society works to inspire future generations of women aviators through educational outreach. The organization provides aviation scholarship opportunities for women seeking a career in aviation.

National Gay Pilots Association (NGPA)
5115 Excelsior Blvd. #475
St. Louis Park, MN 55416
website: www.ngpa.org

This organization focuses on pilots, mechanics, air traffic controllers, flight instructors, and other aviation workers in the lesbian, gay, bisexual, and transgender (LGBT) community. The NGPA advocates for equal treatment of LGBT aviators and encourages members of the community to begin piloting careers. Every year, the group's education fund awards about twelve scholarships worth $5,000 each.

Air Traffic Controller

What Does an Air Traffic Controller Do?

Every day more than eighty-seven thousand flights take off and land at American airports. Air traffic controllers determine the flight paths of every one of these aircraft, from one-engine Cessnas to gigantic Airbus A380s with 820 passengers on board. Air traffic controllers are also called air controllers, flight controllers, and air traffic control officers. They work in air traffic control towers and use highly specialized skills to coordinate the safe, efficient flow of air traffic. Air controllers use communications equipment, radar, computers, and binoculars while making split-second decisions to ensure the safety of each aircraft. Their job is stressful, but these individuals have the knack to work well under pressure.

The term *juggle* is apt when describing an air traffic controller's duties. Like a juggler keeping numerous balls in the air at once, air controllers simultaneously guide numerous aircraft in and out of airport airspace. Air controllers communicate important information to pilots, giving them clearance to take off and land. Air controllers provide information about air traffic, weather conditions, runway closures, and emergencies. Air traffic controllers also manage workers on the ground, ensuring the safety of baggage handlers, ramp agents, and other airport personnel on the tarmac area. While juggling all these duties, air traffic controllers must work extremely efficiently in order to minimize flight delays.

Air traffic controllers are often specialists. Tower controllers work in air traffic control towers, overseeing the movements of aircraft on runways and taxiways. They check flight plans, give pilots clearance for takeoff and landing, and oversee the movement of aircraft and ground personnel in different areas of the airport. Approach and departure controllers work in buildings called terminal radar approach control centers. Their work involves using radar to maintain a safe, minimum distance between aircraft within an airport's airspace, which is 5 miles (8 km) or more out from an air traffic control tower. Approach and departure controllers give pilots permission to enter a controlled airspace while providing weather and other critical information.

When an airplane leaves an airport's airspace, it is handed off to an en route controller. These people work in air route traffic control centers located throughout the country. En route controllers pay special attention to descending aircraft as they get closer to airports. They may advise a pilot to adjust an aircraft's flight path and altitude to fly around a storm system or avoid a collision. On the So You Want My Job website, air controller Chris Solomon explained how controllers in different positions work with one another:

> The typical tower controllers get the planes from the gate to the runway and then airborne to within 5 or so miles of an airport. The aircraft then becomes under the control of the approach controllers. The approach controllers usually control the aircraft . . . within about 60 miles of an airport. After going above 18,000 [feet], the aircraft is then in the [en route] controller's airspace and is taken across the higher altitudes to the plane's destination.

Some air traffic controllers work at the Air Traffic Control System Command Center in Warrenton, Virginia, which oversees the entire national air flight system. The center's controllers observe the traffic patterns of the four thousand to six thousand aircraft that may be flying in the nation's airspace at any given moment during peak daytime hours. They focus on keeping traffic levels manageable for airport and en route controllers. When a "traffic jam" is expected, controllers at the command center issue orders, changing flight paths to minimize problems.

Working as an air traffic controller is both exciting and challenging. Because lives are at risk when mistakes are made, air controllers must bring their A game to work on every shift, which means remaining constantly focused and vigilant. But this can make the job extremely stressful. Controllers spend their days juggling aircraft in flight and on the ground. Losing track of the position of any one of these aircraft could be disastrous. As air traffic controller Ron Connolly told CNN: "You can have an extremely intense day, where you can actually hear your heart pounding in your ears while you're working." The intense concentration required to keep planes landing in a safe and orderly fashion has been compared to playing Ping-Pong with ten people at once. The problem is aggravated by staff shortages at some of the nation's busiest airports, such as those in Atlanta, Chicago, and Houston, where controllers often work six-day workweeks. Because of the stress associated with the job, about 10 percent of air traffic controllers leave the job every year because of mental and physical burnout.

How Do You Become an Air Traffic Controller?

In 2013 the Federal Aviation Administration (FAA) initiated the Air Traffic Controller Workforce Plan to hire and train over ten thousand air traffic controllers with no previous air traffic control experience. In 2016 the FAA announced that it had hired about 1,350 air controllers since the plan was implemented. The FAA said it would hire 7,400 more by 2021. With this plan, the FAA opened its hiring to the general public. This is notable since the FAA previously only hired those with military experience or students who graduated with a degree as an air traffic controller from an FAA-approved college. According to an FAA announcement on the Air Traffic Controller Workforce Plan website, the program is intended to add "more depth and diversity to our controller hiring sources." In order to be accepted to the FAA training program, applicants must be able to pass the difficult Air Traffic Selection and Training exam, which tests for skills necessary to become an air traffic controller. Applicants must also demonstrate abilities in math, prioritizing tasks, and planning. Furthermore, they must show they can work in a high-stress environment.

Because air traffic control positions are government jobs, applicants must be US citizens. Prospective air controllers must be able to speak clear English so they can be understood over electronic radio equipment. Additionally, qualified applicants are required to pass rigorous medical and psychological tests. Prospective air controllers must also pass a security clearance, which means they must have a clean record; applicants with serious financial issues, convictions for driving while intoxicated, or criminal charges relating to firearms, domestic violence, or drugs may not qualify. Given the stress of the job and the heightened fears of terrorism, the FAA wants individuals who have a spotless background with no known patterns of erratic behavior. Finally, applicants can be no older than thirty-one when they begin their careers as air traffic controllers.

Education

A person does not need a college degree to be an air traffic controller. However, many job candidates choose to attend a community college that offers an FAA-approved air traffic control program called the Air Traffic Collegiate Training Initiative. The program offers two- and four-year nonengineering aviation degrees that include basic courses in air traffic control and aviation administration.

Training

Most newly hired air traffic controllers are required to take further training at the FAA Academy in Oklahoma City, Oklahoma. The length of the training depends on the candidate's education and previous work experience. Trainees learn FAA rules, regulations, and standardized procedures used in air traffic control. They study weather guidelines, control communications, aircraft recognition, emergency procedures, and tower operations. When these courses are completed, students take tower qualification training, which combines computer simulation and training in an actual control tower.

After graduation from the academy, trainees work as developmental controllers in air traffic control facilities. As developmental controllers, trainees supply basic flight data and airport information to pilots. In time, they advance to positions with greater responsibility, such as en route controllers. With additional training, developmental controllers can move to positions in air control towers.

Certification and Licensing

All air traffic controllers must hold an air traffic control tower operator certificate. In order to keep the certificate, controllers must undergo physical and mental exams each year, take job performance exams twice a year, and submit to periodic drug tests.

Skills and Personality

Communication skills are paramount for air traffic controllers; they spend their days issuing clear, concise instructions to pilots, ground crews, and others while listening, absorbing, and quickly processing information received from airline personnel. Organizational skills are also important since air controllers coordinate the movements of multiple flights, guiding several pilots at once. Air controllers must be able to concentrate under pressure and to think in the noisy environment of an air control tower, where everyone is talking at the same time. They must be able to make quick decisions when instructing pilots heading into bad weather or dealing with emergencies. Since air controllers constantly monitor distances and flight speeds, they need a good grasp of math. As Solomon told So You Want My Job, "If I was building a controller, I'd say the top 5 things I'd put in would be being able to think on your feet in stressful situations, the ability to make sound decisions, ability to take criticism, systematic thinking, and the ability to have fun while you're working."

Employers

Air traffic controllers work for the FAA, staffing its 315 air traffic control facilities. Some facilities are the air control towers passengers see at airports. The FAA also maintains radar control centers, where air controllers provide services outside the areas handled by control towers. Air controllers also work at the Air Traffic Control System Command Center operated by the FAA.

Working Conditions

Air controllers typically work five eight-hour shifts every week. However, schedules vary, and workweeks often combine rotating shifts—a day shift, a few nighttime swing shifts, and a few midnight-to-dawn graveyard shifts. This scheduling is hard on workers but justified by the FAA, since major air traffic control centers operate twenty-four hours a day. While most passenger jets do not take off and land late at night, cargo jets for companies like UPS and FedEx typically fly at night. And just like their colleagues who fly passenger jets, cargo pilots need the services of air controllers. While the FAA requires controllers to have nine hours of rest between shifts, many times air controllers operate on as little as four hours' sleep. As Connolly told CNN, "I used to feel that I was so tired that I actually felt sore. . . . It was very difficult to stay awake, extremely difficult." Such statements have attracted the attention of the flying public, forcing the FAA to double up on the number of controllers where possible. And the Air Traffic Controller Workforce Plan is expected to provide some relief by increasing the number of air traffic controllers in the coming years.

Earnings

While working as an air traffic controller might be stressful and exhausting, the job includes a six-figure salary. The median annual wage for air traffic controllers was $122,950 in May 2015. Those who work in small airports might only earn $66,780, but supervisors at large facilities can earn more than $172,590 per year.

Opportunities for Advancement

Air traffic controllers begin their careers as developmental controllers and earn more pay and advance to higher positions with experience. Air traffic controllers with the most experience can become supervisors.

What Is the Future Outlook for Air Traffic Controllers?

According to the Bureau of Labor Statistics, employment for air traffic controllers is expected to decline by 9 percent from 2016 to 2024. While the FAA does not expect to reduce the overall number of controllers in the short term, job opportunities depend on how many workers retire. In the long term, the FAA is working to incorporate the high-tech Next Generation Air Transportation System (NextGen), which will employ satellites to take over some of the duties currently handled by air controllers. While fewer controllers will handle more air traffic, the NextGen system is not expected to be fully operational until after 2025.

Find Out More

AviationEd
PO Box 282
Evanston, IL 60204
website: http://aviationed.net

AviationEd is an organization of aviation and educational professionals committed to inspiring students to pursue careers in aerospace and aviation. The organization runs K–12 school enrichment programs, seasonal camps, and special events featuring hands-on activities geared toward teaching real-world applications related to air traffic control and other aviation fields.

Federal Aviation Administration (FAA)/Aviation Careers
800 Independence Ave. SW
Washington, DC 20591
website: www.faa.gov

The FAA employs all air traffic controllers in the United States. This web page describes the minimum requirements to be an air traffic controller and provides links to pertinent information such as the FAA medical and security requirements and the air traffic preemployment tests.

National Air Traffic Controllers Association (NATCA)
1325 Massachusetts Ave. NW
Washington, DC 20005
website: www.natca.org

The NATCA represents air traffic controllers and other aviation employees, supports air traffic control reform, and works with legislators to ensure stable, predictable funding for the National Airspace System, which oversees airspace and air navigation facilities in the United States. The NATCA offers scholarships to spouses and children of active, retired, and deceased NATCA members.

Virtual Air Traffic Simulation Network (VATSIM)
website: www.vatsim.net

VATSIM is a free online platform that allows virtual pilots to connect their flight simulators into one shared virtual world. VATSIM also simulates air traffic control in the virtual world, creating a hands-on experience for virtual aviation enthusiasts.

Meteorologist

What Does a Meteorologist Do?

When most people think about what a meteorologist does, they probably picture the friendly TV weather forecaster who appears on the local news channel every day. Most, but not all, of these telegenic local celebrities are trained meteorologists. They tell viewers about past and current weather conditions and approaching storms, cold fronts, and heat waves. They usually also forecast weather for the coming week.

Whatever the common notions about meteorologists, only about 7 percent are employed as TV weather broadcasters. The vast majority of meteorologists work in aviation and aerospace. In fact, pilots and ground crews are so dependent on meteorologists that weather forecasters are considered important members of every flight team.

Meteorologists are also known as atmospheric scientists. They study how weather and climate influence human activities and the environment. The work of a meteorologist includes measuring temperature, humidity, wind speed and direction, atmospheric pressure, and other weather-related events. Meteorologists collect and analyze this weather data using basic tools like thermometers to measure temperature, barometers to measure air pressure, hygrometers to gauge humidity, and anemometers to check wind speed. More complex weather forecasting instruments include weather balloons, weather buoys, satellites, radar systems, and computers. The main job of a meteorologist is to interpret the collected data and use it to make hour-to-hour, day-to-day weather forecasts and warnings. This information is issued to airlines, air traffic controllers, airports, pilot information facilities called flight service stations, the National Weather Service (NWS), and the general public. Oftentimes a meteorologist will personally advise a pilot who is drawing up a flight plan.

Meteorologists work in large and small facilities called weather stations. These contain equipment for measuring atmospheric conditions and may be located on land or sea. Those who work in small stations often work alone or with a few others. Small-station meteorologists perform numerous jobs, including making outdoor weather observations, recording information on weather instruments, checking weather data coming in from different regions, creating weather maps, making forecasts, and advising aviators and others. Meteorologists use computers to obtain data and create weather maps, but they also send and receive information by telephone and fax machine.

Meteorologists who work in large weather stations are often specialists. Those with the job title of operational forecaster analyze weather conditions and issue forecasts and weather alerts for severe weather in a specific area. Research meteorologists study a specific type of weather, such as tornadoes or climate change. These professionals also develop software and radar programs, as well as weather models used by other meteorologists. Airline meteorologists use their talents to forecast weather for pilots, who use the information to take off, land, and safely fly across the country while avoiding strong winds and storms.

How Do You Become a Meteorologist?

It is common for meteorologists to say they fell in love with weather forecasting when they were very young. Meteorologist Doug

Kammerer is typical. In 2013 he told the *Washington Post* he picked his career when he was only eight years old. "I love all kinds of weather—thunderstorms, tornadoes, hurricanes, snowstorms," Kammerer said. "I love them all." Individuals who enjoy observing weather phenomena and analyzing complex data, excel at math and science, and want to work with radar, satellites, and other sophisticated equipment can add meteorology to their future career forecast.

Education

Being a meteorologist requires extensive knowledge of math and computers; some meteorologists edit or write their own software programs to produce weather forecasts. Prospective meteorologists can make their high school years count by taking advanced math courses, including statistics and calculus. At the college level, meteorologists need to acquire a bachelor's degree in meteorology or a related earth science such as physics, chemistry, or geology. Those who are interested in a research position work toward obtaining a master's or doctorate degree in atmospheric science. Prospective meteorologists should be advised, though, that meteorology is a very difficult major, with a heavy focus on mathematics, physics, computer programming, and thermodynamics.

Certification and Licensing

There are no requirements for certification and licensing. However, meteorologists who are hired by the NWS must undergo two hundred hours of on-the-job training per year for the first two years of employment.

Volunteer Work and Internships

Many students working to earn a degree in meteorology seek intern positions through the Pathways Program offered by the NWS. The program provides NWS work opportunities to students from high school to graduate level. Students in the program work on important projects focused on meteorology and related areas such as hydrology and biology. Participants also learn how the NWS provides up-to-date weather information to protect and serve the public.

Skills and Personality

Critical-thinking and analytical skills are important to meteorologists; they spend many hours every day working on computers and examining the massive amounts of data used to make forecasts as accurate as possible. These tasks require advanced math skills to develop weather models and understand the relationship between air pressure, temperature, and other weather specifics. Meteorologists also need to listen and speak clearly; pilots, government officials, and others who depend on receiving concise weather information expect meteorologists to have good communication skills.

On the Job

Employers

The NWS, operated by the federal government, is at the center of the meteorology world. The agency operates more than 120 weather forecast offices, which provide weather information and warnings. The NWS operates NEXRAD, a nationwide system of Doppler radars that can detect precipitation and wind conditions. The NWS also operates the National Centers for Environmental Prediction, which oversees numerous weather-related agencies, including the Aviation Weather Center, the Climate Prediction Center, the National Hurricane Center, the Storm Prediction Center, and the Weather Prediction Center.

The space agency NASA is another government agency that employs meteorologists. Before every rocket launch, NASA weather teams closely monitor weather conditions. When a rocket is being prepared, high winds and rain can cause problems for ground crews. When a rocket is about to be launched, the weather must be monitored everywhere from the launch pad to thousands of feet in the air. While speeding rockets leave the atmosphere in only a few minutes, a single low-hanging cloud or high winds in the upper atmosphere can cause problems for a mission. Oftentimes it is the meteorologist who issues the recommendation to halt or delay a mission.

Meteorologists also work for state and local governments; they alert emergency response teams and road crews when severe weather is predicted. When a school is closed for a snow day—or some other weather-related cause—it is thanks to a local government meteorologist.

Some meteorologists work in the private weather forecasting industry providing services that are not in competition with the NWS. For example, a number of private companies design and sell software to present and package forecasts for the media. Meteorologists are also employed by utility companies to predict when heat waves or cold snaps will drive up demand for natural gas and electricity—or when storms might down power lines and create other problems. Agricultural meteorologists provide short- and long-term forecasts for farmers, agribusiness companies, and other food producers. Some teach meteorology in classrooms and conduct research at colleges and universities.

Weather modeling and private weather forecasting are the two main areas of growth in meteorology. Those involved in weather modeling use mathematical models of the atmosphere and ocean to predict weather based on current conditions. These models are integrated and customized for use in private industry. For example, an offshore oil-drilling company needs different weather models than a construction company. Private forecasters mostly work for large companies like Climate Corporation and StormGeo, which provide professional weather services to agriculture, hospitality, construction, and other industries.

Perhaps the most exciting—and rare—job for a meteorologist is to work as a storm chaser, researching and seeking to document the behavior of tornadoes and other extreme weather systems. In an interview with *Popular Mechanics*, Emily Sutton, an Oklahoma meteorologist, described chasing her first tornado: "It was just a rush to see this unpredictable force of nature form before your eyes, and seeing how beautiful it is, but at the same time you know how destructive it could be."

Working Conditions

Meteorologists work outdoors when making weather observations and checking instruments, but they spend most of their time indoors. They might sit at desks or stand at map tables while working on weather maps and charts. Since airports are active twenty-four hours a day, meteorologists—especially entry-level workers—often work in rotating shifts. They might work a few day shifts, a nighttime swing shift, and a few overnight graveyard shifts. Meteorologists also work holidays and weekends. Overtime work is also required during weather emergencies like hurricanes, snowstorms, and tornadoes. And since weather can change suddenly, there is little downtime; in most climates, meteorologists must monitor conditions constantly.

Earnings

Meteorology is a very competitive field. For every position available at the NWS, there are one hundred applicants. And the pay is not great. The beginning annual salary for NWS applicants with a bachelor's degree in meteorology is around $30,000. Forecasters who have successful yearly management reviews have a potential income of $60,000 to $100,000 per year. Management-level positions can pay up to $120,000 per year. The median annual salary for meteorologists is $89,820, about the same amount earned by a weather forecaster on TV.

Opportunities for Advancement

Meteorologists with advanced degrees have a much better chance of finding advanced employment opportunities and obtaining higher salaries. For example, a meteorologist with a master's degree in business administration can work as a consultant for a private firm, such as an insurance company, that needs accurate forecasts to make important business decisions. Meteorology programmers—those with excellent computer programming skills—are in high demand and have ample opportunities to advance their careers. As meteorologist A.J. Jain explained on his *Fresh AJ Weather Blog*, "Whether it is programming using Python, C++, Objective C, or PHP. . . . Some [private employers are] prepared to throw ridiculous amounts of cash [at you] if you met those qualifications."

What Is the Future Outlook for Meteorologists?

Opportunities for meteorologists are expected to grow 9 percent by 2024—faster than average for other fields. Much of this growth will be in the private sector as more businesses come to rely on what is called just-in-time (JIT) delivery; the strategy is employed by companies that keep inventory levels low to avoid expenses such as building large warehouses and hiring employees to work in them. A JIT company orders supplies only when they are needed, but severe weather can interrupt deliveries and temporarily shut down production. To avoid this, JIT businesses are increasingly relying on forecasting teams to advise inventory workers to help them keep supplies flowing.

Find Out More

American Meteorological Society (AMS)
45 Beacon St.
Boston, MA 02108
website: www.ametsoc.org

The AMS promotes and broadcasts information about the weather sciences. Its members include scientists, researchers, educators, broadcast meteorologists, and students. The Education and Careers link on the AMS website includes resources for students from kindergarten to college and offers listings for internships and jobs.

Climate Central
154 Grand St.
New York, NY 10013
website: www.climatecentral.org

This organization is dedicated to communicating the science and effects of climate change to meteorologists, researchers, and the general public. The website contains numerous articles, studies, and reports about extreme weather trends like storms and droughts, and provides job listings for meteorologists and others in the field.

National Severe Storms Laboratory (NSSL)
120 David L. Boren Blvd.
Norman, OK 73072
website: www.nssl.noaa.gov

The NSSL is a federal weather research lab that studies severe weather in order to improve warnings and forecasts, save lives, and reduce property damage. The organization's website has numerous learning resources for the public, students, and educators and provides links to pages offering undergraduate research and job opportunities, scholarships, and postdoctoral fellowships.

National Weather Service (NWS)
1325 East West Highway
Silver Spring, MD 20910
website: www.weather.gov

The NWS employs over four thousand people. The agency provides forecasts, warnings, and weather, water, and climate data to government agencies, industries, and the general public. The Careers link on the website contains information about NWS internships available to students enrolled in a wide variety of educational institutions, from high school to graduate level.

Planetary Scientist

What Does a Planetary Scientist Do?

In August 2011 NASA launched the *Juno* space probe to study the physical makeup of the planet Jupiter. After a faultless flight of 540 million miles (869 million km), the *Juno* probe entered Jupiter's orbit on July 4, 2016. *Juno*'s mission involves flying around the planet until February 2018, when it will nose-dive into the Jovian atmosphere and burn up. The entire $1.1 billion *Juno* mission was driven by a quest to further humanity's knowledge of planetary science. Little wonder planetary scientists were among the dozens of cheering people in the Mission Juno control room on July 4.

Juno is chock-full of instrumentation designed by planetary scientists to further their work. Planetary scientists were involved in the construction of *Juno*'s microwave radiometer, which measures the quantities of ammonia and water in the atmosphere. Planetary scientists are closely watching *Juno*'s magnetometer in order to map Jupiter's powerful magnetic fields. Other instruments will investigate Jupiter's wild winds, which can reach speeds of 384 miles per hour (618 kph). The probe also carries a camera that will send pictures of Jupiter's poles and clouds back to scientists on Earth.

Information collected from *Juno*'s scientific instruments will tell planetary scientists about Jupiter's role in the formation of the solar system and help prove complex theories that will help scientists understand various physical properties of Earth. The *Juno* probe might also reveal the existence of alien microbes living in the solar system. Planetary scientist Guy Beutelschies was all smiles in a video NASA released after *Juno* reached the giant planet: "Putting an orbiter around Jupiter is why we all go into this profession; it's science fiction and yet it's fact."

Those who work as planetary scientists use data and photos from space missions to study the features of planets, moons, asteroids, comets, and interplanetary dust within the solar system (but not the sun). Planetary scientists might construct digital 3-D models to study the environment of Olympus Mons on Mars—the highest mountain in the solar system. Or they might dissect high-definition photos of Mercury's frozen ice craters sent back to Earth in 2014 by the *Messenger* spacecraft.

Whatever their field of interest, planetary scientists try to crack the mysteries of the planets. Planetary science student A. Solé Carretero explained the importance of the work in a blog for the International Space University website: "Planetary science may in the not too-distant future end up revealing that our planet is in fact not so unique, that life exists and can thrive in other planetary bodies of our solar system or of other solar systems."

Most people who work in aerospace and aviation can see the results of their work on a regular basis. Pilots take satisfaction in completing a flawless flight; engineers are gratified when a piece of equipment they designed is tested and installed in an aircraft. But those who work as planetary scientists are in it for the long haul. Their work is demanding and involves deep knowledge of complex science, from biology to engineering and physics. Planetary scientists might have to wait ten to fifteen years before a spacecraft is launched to complete their mission. If the launch is successful, like the *Juno* mission, a probe can take five to seven years to reach its destination, where failure is a constant threat due to the extreme environments found in outer space.

Beyond the technical complexities, planetary scientists have to deal with political and social realities. Most planetary scientists say the biggest threat to their work comes from budget cuts. This means scientists often have to convince politicians and government officials to provide grants for complex projects with complicated goals. And even when projects are moving forward, scientists are required to spend many hours dealing with paperwork and bureaucracy.

Planetary scientists also have to navigate the politics of working as members of a large team populated with international partners from different cultures. This requires team members to build bridges across language and cultural chasms. Many planetary scientists also take on the work of educating the public and inspiring the next generation of scientists. This means visiting classrooms, giving lectures, and working to promote planetary science through outreach and communications programs.

How Do You Become a Planetary Scientist?

Most planetary scientists say they became interested in space exploration, star gazing, and science fiction stories at a young age. In an interview with the NASA Quest! website, Jennifer Heldmann explained what inspired her to become a planetary scientist. "I remember that we learned about the planets one day in third grade and from then I was hooked," she said. "My friend introduced me to the movie *Space Camp* when I was 10 years old and after that we would set up our own shuttle 'cockpit' and re-enact the mission from lift-off to landing."

However, becoming a planetary scientist involves much more than loving Saturn or *Space Camp*; it is one of the most complex career paths a person can choose. By the time Heldmann entered high school, she was learning all she could about astronomy, the geological composition of the planets, and the physics of spaceflight. As Heldmann told NASA Quest!, "Working hard in school was definitely critical to preparing me for my job. I also learned how to work effectively on my own, as well as in a group, which is very important."

Education

Planetary science is a diverse field that can involve studying in a chemistry, physics, or biology department and mastering a number of complex subjects such as astrobiology, astrophysics, astrochemistry, geochemistry, geophysics, planet dynamics, space plasma physics, and volcanology. Most entry-level positions for planetary scientists require applicants to have at least a master's degree in geology, astronomy, physics, or chemistry. Most in this competitive field hold a PhD in subjects related to planetary sciences, such as applied physics, astronomy, astrophysics, or geochemistry. A glance at Heldmann's training on NASA Quest! provides a good example of a planetary scientist's education. She got a bachelor of science degree in astro-geophysics at Colgate University in New York, a master of science in space studies with a minor in geology at the University of North Dakota, and a PhD in planetary science at the University of Colorado.

Volunteer Work and Internships

Numerous institutions offer internships, fellowships, and scholarships to those with an interest in planetary science. NASA Pathways Programs provide opportunities to students and recent college graduates. The Lunar and Planetary Institute, near Johnson Space Center in Houston, Texas, offers programs to undergraduates with at least fifty semester hours to conduct cutting-edge research in planetary sciences. The Scientific and Engineering Student Internship Program at the Goddard Space Flight Center in Greenbelt, Maryland, offers summer jobs to students. And the Jet Propulsion Laboratory in Pasadena, California, offers a Planetary Science Summer School program.

Skills and Personality

Planetary scientists draw on enthusiasm, intelligence, and creativity to pursue confounding puzzles related to the earth sciences, math, physics, and more. They are expected to be the best and brightest in their respective fields. And since they work in large teams, they must also exhibit humility and a spirit of cooperation. Teamwork was mentioned by Fran Bagenal, an expert in plasma physics, who gave an interview to the *Women in Planetary Science* blog. She said, "Getting on with people is . . . important—perhaps as important as solving big equations." Beyond brilliance and teamwork, patience is truly a virtue for a planetary scientist, whose day-to-day efforts might not come to fruition for years or even decades. Additionally, since planetary scientists often work with colleagues from France, Japan, Russia, China, India, and other nations, it is helpful to be fluent in at least one foreign language.

On the Job

Employers

Most planetary scientists teach at universities and take on work as independent contractors for NASA and research facilities like the Jet Propulsion Laboratory. Those with experience might move between these institutions at various times during their careers. For example, Bagenal is a professor of astrophysical and planetary sciences at the University of Colorado who also works with NASA on the *Juno* mission and conducts research at the Jet Propulsion Laboratory. As Bagenal told *Women in Planetary Science*, "It's a great job! And there are all sorts of jobs—mission design, mission operations, data analysis, modeling."

Working Conditions

Planetary scientists work in many settings, from classrooms to laboratories to mission control rooms at NASA. Most work forty-hour weeks, but at the culmination of major projects, planetary scientists might work up to twenty hours a day. Some take time off from work to conduct research outdoors in extreme environments.

Earnings

About twenty thousand people worked as planetary scientists in 2015, and the field was expected to grow by 7 percent by 2024. A planetary scientist straight out of college can earn around $69,040 a year doing basic research. Those with experience in atmospherics and general space sciences can expect a salary of $81,289, while physicists and as-tronomers have an annual median income of $110,000.

Opportunities for Advancement

Planetary scientists depend on NASA and other federal agencies to provide money through research grants. This means planetary scientists spend a significant portion of their time writing grant proposals, seeking funds to study a single question or number of questions pertaining to the solar system or a particular planet. The competition is fierce, and NASA only accepts about 10 percent of grant requests. The grants usually last three years but rarely pay a scientist's entire salary, let alone the full cost of equipment and the salaries of graduate students employed as research assistants. This means planetary scientists must work on two or three grants at a time. Casey Dreier, a planetary scientist who blogs for the Planetary Society website, explains the toll this can take on scientists: "If you know scientists (or follow some on Twitter) you'll notice that a few times a year they'll start to get pretty distracted. They'll start looking haggard, maybe they'll have big bags under their eyes, or develop stress lines, or just disappear from view for a while. When asked, they'll say something vague about working on a 'proposal.' This is grant-writing time." Grant rejection is a particular problem for early-career scientists. Those with more experience are looked on more favorably by grant money providers. Planetary scientists with the most experience can find jobs at NASA and work full-time on major projects like Mission Juno.

What Is the Future Outlook for Planetary Scientists?

While employment in the field of planetary science is expected to grow at an average rate of 7 percent until 2024, about half of all planetary scientists receive funding through NASA's $250 million research and analysis budget. NASA's budget is often on the chopping block, and future employment for planetary scientists depends on the space agency receiving adequate funding. This is far from guaranteed in the foreseeable future.

Find Out More

Astrogeology Science Center
2255 N. Gemini Dr.
Flagstaff, AZ 86001
website: http://astrogeology.usgs.gov

The Astrogeology Science Center, operated by the US Geological Survey, works with NASA and other space agencies to select rover landing sites, create maps of the planets, and conduct research on the makeup of various planetary surfaces. The staff often works together with students and interns who can apply for programs on the center's website.

Division for Planetary Sciences (DPS)
1667 K St. NW, Suite 800
Washington, DC 20006
website: https://dps.aas.org

The DPS is a division of the American Astronomical Society, a professional organization of physicists, mathematicians, geologists, engineers, and astronomers. The website offers information about education planning, internships, and careers in planetary science.

International Astronautical Federation (IAF)
3 rue Mario Nikis
75015 Paris, France
website: www.iafastro.org

The IAF advocates for space exploration and international cooperation between scientists, space agencies, aerospace companies, and related associations. The federation supports numerous education and young professionals' activities, such as the Emerging Space Leaders Grant Programme, the Young Space Leaders Recognition Programme, and the IAF Student Competition.

Planetary Science Institute (PSI)
1700 E. Fort Lowell, Suite 106
Tucson, AZ 85719
website: www.psi.edu

The PSI is the largest nongovernment employer of planetary scientists in the world. The institute's members are involved in science education and fieldwork. The PSI offers professional development workshops, undergraduate internships, virtual tours of craters, and a meteorite rock kit with real samples.

Astronaut

At a Glance:

Astronaut

Minimum Educational Requirements

Bachelor's degree in engineering, biological sciences, physical sciences, computer science, or math; three years' professional experience obtained after degree completion, which can include obtaining a master's or doctorate degree, OR three years or 1,000 hours as a jet aircraft pilot-in-command

Personal Qualities

Intelligence, bravery, calm under pressure, physical endurance, ability to conduct research experiments, ability to operate as an aircraft pilot or crew

Certification and Licensing

Pilot astronauts are required to be licensed jet airplane pilots with 1,000 hours' flight experience

Working Conditions

Astronauts study in classrooms, train in land and water survival facilities, and work in the dangerous environment of outer space.

Salary Range

In 2015, $66,026 to $158,700 per year

Number of Jobs

99 in 2015

Future Job Outlook

Little change in the number of people working as astronauts in the coming years

What Does an Astronaut Do?

In 2011 when Marist Poll conducted its annual opinion survey, it asked American kids what they wanted to be when they grew up. For the first time in over forty years, "astronaut" was not listed in the top ten dream jobs for kids, most of whom daydreamed of becoming actors, athletes, or tech titans. Back in the 1960s and early 1970s, when NASA launched major space missions every year—and landed on the moon—millions of kids fantasized about becoming astronauts. Astronauts were the superheroes of the day, donning their crinkly spacesuits, strapping themselves into tiny modules fitted to the tips of monstrous rockets, and soaring away from Earth in a giant ball of flame. In 1969, when Neil Armstrong and Buzz Aldrin became the first humans to walk on the moon, nearly everyone in the world with a

TV watched the event unfold. Although the last moon walk occurred in December 1972, kids continued to tell pollsters they wanted to be astronauts well into the 2000s. While the job might not be as popular as it once was, it is still possible to become an astronaut, although the odds are about one in six hundred.

Since 1958 NASA has trained astronauts extensively to pilot spacecraft, travel through space, conduct spacewalks, and walk on the moon. There are two types of astronauts at NASA. Mission specialists conduct experiments, maintain spacecraft and equipment, and launch satellites. They might also work on the ground, training astronaut candidates. Pilot astronauts are responsible for commanding space shuttles and the International Space Station (ISS) while overseeing the crew, mission, and safety of the flight.

How Do You Become an Astronaut?

Every four to five years, NASA hires new people for its Astronaut Corps, and there is never a shortage of qualified candidates. During the last round of hiring in 2013, the agency received 6,372 applications, a record number. Eight lucky hopefuls were picked to form Group 21 of the Astronaut Corps. This was not the finish line for their dream; it was the starting gate. These astronauts trained nonstop for two years before they were made available for space missions, and there is no guarantee they will ever set foot in a spacecraft.

For members of Group 21, like the other groups before them, receiving NASA training was the culmination of many years of education and hard work. One member of the group, Josh A. Cassada, was a lieutenant commander in the navy with a PhD in particle physics. Anne McClain was a major in the army who piloted attack helicopters in 216 combat missions in Iraq. She also has a master's degree in engineering. Jessica Meir is a Harvard professor with a master's degree in space studies. Needless to say, one needs focus and dedication to join this elite group of astronauts.

Those with the education and skills to become candidates for the Astronaut Corps spend the first week attending personal interviews and medical and physiological screenings. Once completed, the candidates are sent to Houston for training at NASA's Johnson Space Center. In an interview with CBS News, McClain described the initial training by stating, "No matter what your background is coming in, you're going to have to learn and master things that you've never seen before." Things that need to be mastered include preparing for an emergency space capsule splashdown in water. This requires astronauts to take difficult swim tests and learn to tread water for extended periods of time in a flight suit and running shoes. There is also underwater training, in which astronauts practice for spacewalks in giant water tanks.

Astronauts also prepare extensively for living in the zero-gravity conditions of outer space. This training is conducted during three-hour flights in large cargo jets with padded walls. The jet climbs and descends rapidly at a 45-degree angle, which provides a few seconds of zero gravity for the crew. This up-and-down process occurs around

NASA Commander Terry Virts works on a blood pressure experiment in a laboratory aboard the International Space Station in 2015. Depending on their specialty, astronauts might conduct experiments, maintain spacecraft and equipment, launch satellites, or oversee missions.

forty times on a typical flight, causing many trainees to experience air-sickness. For this reason, the aircraft is nicknamed the "vomit comet."

Those who graduate from the candidate program are required to complete training in robotic skills, aircraft flight readiness, ISS systems, and extravehicular activities (for walking in space outside the ISS). Because the ISS is a joint venture with Russia, astronauts are required to learn Russian. The days are long and the work brutal. As McClain told CBS, the initial training is "kind of like being in grad school and boot camp at the same time."

Education

NASA requires members of its Astronaut Corps to have a minimum of a bachelor's degree in mathematics, physical science, biological science, or engineering. In addition, astronaut pilots must work as a pilot-in-command on a jet aircraft for three years or one thousand hours, whichever comes first. For those who are not pilots, NASA requires three years of professional experience, which can include acquiring a master's or doctorate degree. Teachers are in luck when it comes to this requirement; teaching at the kindergarten through high school level for three years qualifies as professional experience.

NASA also has physical requirements for the job. Short people—and tall people—need not apply; astronauts must be at least five feet two inches and no taller than six feet three inches. Astronaut applicants must also pass a NASA long-duration spaceflight physical, which is similar to a military physical. The average age for astronauts is thirty-four, but NASA will hire astronauts between ages twenty-six and forty-six.

For those who fail to make the cut for NASA's Astronaut Corps, a career as an astronaut can be pursued through a private company called Astronauts4Hire. The nonprofit company was formed in 2010 to recruit and train qualified scientists and engineers for spaceflight. In 2016 the all-volunteer membership organization had 170 members.

Volunteer Work and Internships

NASA offers numerous internships to undergrads, graduate students, and postdoctoral researchers. Students are entered into a general applicant pool when they apply to NASA research facilities around the country. Summer internships last ten weeks and pay $6,500. The internships might focus on anything from rocket propulsion to the search for life on alien planets, and numerous current astronauts participated in the program when they were in college.

Skills and Personality

From the beginning of the space program, successful astronauts have been said to have "the right stuff." While the meaning has changed since the 1960s, when most astronauts were hard-charging jet fighter pilots, astronaut candidates today are still expected to have nearly superhuman qualities. They must be brilliant scholars—high achievers at the top of their field—with exceptional physical and psychological endurance that allows them to tolerate the challenges of being in space. They must also be team players to make space missions successful.

On the Job

Employers

NASA is the world's most prominent astronaut employer; in 2016 there were 80 men and women who were members of the NASA Astronaut Corps. An additional 19 were international active astronauts who came from other countries. This number is down from the peak in 2000, when 149 people were in the Astronaut Corps.

Until recently, those who did not make the cut at NASA would have to abandon their space dreams to pursue another career. But today more private companies are getting into the space business, which opens up a few more options for those who want to be astronauts. A Netherlands-based company called Mars One is recruiting astronauts for several missions to the red planet beginning in 2026. When the Mars One project was announced in 2012, the company received nearly 203,000 applications, from which one hundred hopefuls—fifty men and fifty women—were picked. In 2016 this group was pared down to forty astronauts. Mars One is planning to have twenty colonists on Mars by 2035. But before filling out the paperwork, interested parties might want to consider this: The Mars One mission is a one-way trip. Those who journey the 143 million miles (230 million km) will never return to Earth.

Working Conditions

From the minute astronauts climb aboard launch rockets to the minute they return to Earth, they are putting their lives at risk. Space disasters have killed eighteen American astronauts and four Russian cosmonauts—equal to 5 percent of all people who have been in space.

The majority of astronauts live to complete their missions, and the ultimate goal for most is to spend time on board the ISS. The space station floats 250 miles (402 km) above Earth and, at 32,333 cubic feet (916 cu m), is the size of a Boeing 747 jumbo jet. Working conditions in the ISS are far more difficult than any encountered on Earth; the space station is noisy, uncomfortable, and often too hot or too cold. The astronauts' workday on the ISS begins when the NASA ground crew sounds the alarm at 6:00 a.m. The shift includes three meals and 2.5 hours of exercise and ends at 9:30 p.m. Crews spend their days running experiments, cleaning, and conducting maintenance checks and repairs on the station. Sometimes astronauts take spacewalks to conduct repairs outside the ISS. Each detail is carefully mapped a month in advance.

Any accident in outer space can be deadly, and astronauts are wary of three main dangers: fire, depressurization, and toxic spills. Faulty wiring can start fires, and toxic spills (mostly from experiments) can create poisonous clouds of gas that cannot be contained. The biggest fear is depressurization through collision with floating space junk, which travels at 175,000 miles per hour (281,635 kph). There are millions of pieces of old rockets and satellites floating in Earth orbit, and NASA constantly monitors this debris, notifying crews to move the ISS in order to prevent accidents. Added to all the dangers, astronauts spend months away from family and friends in an environment where they cannot feel the sun on their faces or the wind in their hair.

Earnings

NASA Astronaut Corps recruits are paid an annual salary of $66,026, while those with the most experience at the space agency can earn $158,700. Astronauts who are also members of the military remain on active duty and receive their full pay and benefits.

Opportunities for Advancement

Those who are selected as astronaut candidates are promoted to the Astronaut Corps. Once designated an astronaut, there is little opportunity for advancement, although one member of the team gets to act as crew chief.

What Is the Future Outlook for Astronauts?

In December 2015 NASA placed a want ad on the government-run USAJOBS website for an unspecified number of new astronaut candidates. According to the NASA ad, "Today, more new human spacecraft are in development in the United States than at any time in history, and future Astronaut Candidates will have the opportunity to explore farther in space than humans have ever been." The ad explained where the candidates might work; they might fly to the ISS, serve on two commercial spacecraft under construction by private companies, or find a spot on NASA's *Orion* deep-space exploration vehicle, set to begin missions around 2020. While NASA continues to search for new astronaut candidates, it is unlikely the number of active astronauts will increase in coming years. The odds of becoming an astronaut are long.

Find Out More

Association of Space Explorers (ASE)
141 Bay Area Blvd.
Webster, TX 77598
website: www.space-explorers.org

The ASE represents current and former astronauts and promotes the global benefits of space exploration, international cooperation in space missions, and the education of a new generation of astronauts. ASE scholarships are available to students who wish to pursue a career in space science, engineering, or space business administration.

NASAPeople: Astronaut Selection Program
300 E St. SW, Suite 5R30
Washington, DC 20546
website: http://astronauts.nasa.gov

This website explains NASA's criteria for hiring astronauts and provides information about hiring schedules and training. For those who want to fly into outer space, this is the place to begin.

National Space Society (NSS)
PO Box 98106
Washington, DC 20090-8106
website: www.nss.org

The NSS is a grassroots educational organization with members that include current and retired astronauts. The NSS website contains information about space news, tourism, transportation, and policy. The organization sponsors the Enterprise in Space contest, which sends student experiments into Earth orbit on the ISS and brings them back.

Planetary Society
60 S. Los Robles Ave.
Pasadena, CA 91101
website: www.planetary.org

This organization, founded by Bill Nye, advocates for space exploration and funds student projects aimed at developing innovative space technologies. The site contains comprehensive multimedia information about space and the planets, and it features blogs by Nye and other space educators.

Interview with an Aerospace Engineer

Ted Stern is a San Diego aerospace engineer who has been developing solar power systems for spacecraft and satellites for twenty-five years. His job title with Alliance Spacesystems is director of Solar Power Solutions. Stern spoke with the author about his career by text message.

Q: Why did you become an engineer in the aerospace field?

A: I was always excited about the prospects of exploring space—with humans, spacecraft, and robots. And I enjoyed learning how computers can perceive and simulate real-life situations in outer space.

Q: What does a director of Solar Power Solutions do?

A: I develop solar power systems for satellites, the only practical source of electricity in space—obviously we can't run an extension cord from the earth, and other sources of electricity, batteries and fuel, have very limited duration. The systems I develop are light and durable enough to be launched. They can effectively operate and survive in the very harsh environments of space. Some solar systems are used for space exploration but most are used to power spacecraft for commercial use, such as the ones that allows me to text you right now. The satellites can also provide observations from space that can, for example, tell a farmer when to water his crops by measuring moisture in his soil from pictures taken from space.

Q: Can you describe your typical workday?

A: A typical workday for me involves leading a team of engineers who custom design and analyze solar panels for specific customers. Solving problems like how do we make the panels light enough and small enough to fit into the payload bay of the launch vehicle. And how do we make sure that protons and electrons, and intense UV light, heat and cold in space don't damage the panels. The space environment is not very friendly but that is a fun challenge. We have a lot of design tools at our disposal for solving these problems. We use computer aided design (CAD) and computer modeling packages like Satellite Tool Kit (STK)—students can download a free version of STK to play with.

Q: What do you like most about your job?

A: Engineering is about solving problems using technology. It's a fun challenge and the technology is cool. Seeing something being tested and passing the tests can be very exciting too. We have special chambers for thermal vacuum and radiation testing and it's gratifying when you test a piece of hardware and your design solution works. Working in teams is an important part of my job and collaborating with others is stimulating and fun too.

Q: What do you like least about your job?

A: I work in private industry so making a profit is important to our survival as an organization. We have demanding customers and owners who put a lot of pressure on us to work quickly, accurately, and efficiently. It can sometimes be frustrating when customers and business owners make unreasonable demands for performance. Or when the bankers who fund this and every manufacturing industry care only about the bottom line. Of course they have their own pressures.

Q: Are other sectors better to work in?

A: Outside private industry it is possible to work for the public sector (NASA and Air Force Space Command, for example) or for academia (Caltech's Jet Propulsion Lab, or the Johns Hopkins University Applied Physics Lab). Those sectors have their own frustrations and their own benefits as well I'm sure.

Q: What personal qualities do you find most valuable for this type of work?

A: To be successful one should have attention to detail, a positive attitude and a good work ethic. There are rewards—we are well-paid professionals—but this is not a get rich quick job. Slow and steady wins the race—time management is key. Good communication and documentation skills are also needed to write technical prose and effective PowerPoint presentations; a solid foundation of computer skills in Excel and the ability to learn other technical apps such as Matlab is also important. Additionally, good interpersonal skills are necessary to deal with smart self-assured people. And most importantly, you need the ability to reason through difficult situations with calm grace.

Q: What advice do you have for students who might be interested in this career?

A: Get a broad education as an undergrad—take basic courses in multiple disciplines—physics/mechanics as well as a variety of engineering—electrical engineering, mechanical engineering, computer science. Read technical journals and join a technical society such as the American Institute for Aeronautics and Astronautics (AIAA), the Institute of Electrical and Electronics Engineers (IEEE), or the American Society of Mechanical Engineers (ASME). Get involved in projects and develop technical hobbies you find fun—remote control airplanes, app development, robotics—figure out what is fun for you. After all, you will spend 50,000 plus hours of your lifetime working in your engineering profession—you will want to have fun with it. So final piece of advice—have fun with it!!!

Other Careers in Aviation and Aerospace

Aircraft mechanic	Hardware developer
Airway transportation systems specialist	Image scientist
	Instrumentation technician
Astronomer	Lab technician
Aviation safety inspector	Machinist
Avionics technician	Mathematician
Cartographer	Metallurgist
Chemist	Paint technician
Composites technician	Physicist
Cost estimator	Planetary geologist
Database administrator	Propulsion technician
Drafter	Reliability and safety technician
Electrical designer	Research scientist
Electromechanical technician	Sheet metal technician
Electron beam welder	Technical writer/editor
Flight attendant	Telecommunications technician
Flight engineer	Test coordinator
Geophysicist	Toolmaker

Editor's Note: The US Department of Labor's Bureau of Labor Statistics provides information about hundreds of occupations. The agency's *Occupational Outlook Handbook* describes what these jobs entail, the work environment, education and skill requirements, pay, future outlook, and more. The *Occupational Outlook Handbook* may be accessed online at www.bls.gov/ooh.

Index

Note: Boldface page numbers indicate illustrations.

Accreditation Board for
  Engineering and Technology
  (ABET), 22
aerodynamics, 9
aerospace engineer, 11
  advancement opportunities, 14
  certification/licensing, 8, 12
  educational requirements, 8,
    10–12
  employers of, 13
  future job outlook, 8, 14
  information resources, 15
  interview with, 71–73
  number of jobs, 8
  role of, 8–10
  salary/earnings, 8, 14
  skills/personal qualities, 8, 13
  volunteer work/internships,
    12–13
  working conditions, 8, 13–14
aerospace engineering/operations
  technician
  advancement opportunities, 21
  certification/licensing, 16, 19
  educational requirements, 16,
    18–19
  employers of, 20
  future job outlook, 16, 21–22
  information resources, 22–23
  number of jobs, 16
  role of, 16–18
  salary/earnings, 16, 21

  skills/personal qualities, 16,
    19–20
  volunteer work/internships, 19
  working conditions, 16, 20–21
aircraft and avionics equipment
  mechanic, 28
  advancement opportunities, 30
  certification/licensing, 24, 29
  educational requirements, 24,
    27–28
  employers of, 30
  future job outlook, 24, 31
  information resources, 31
  number of jobs, 24
  role of, 24–27
  salary/earnings, 24, 30
  skills/personal qualities, 24, 29
  working conditions, 24, 30
Aircraft Electronics Association
  (AEA), 31
Aircraft Owners and Pilots
  Association (AOPA), 38
airframe and power plant (A&P)
  mechanic, 25–26
Air Line Pilots Association
  (ALPA), 35, 39
Airmen Certification, 16, 19
air traffic controller
  advancement opportunities, 46
  certification/licensing, 40, 44
  educational requirements, 40, 43
  employers of, 45
  future job outlook, 40, 46
  information resources, 46–47
  number of jobs, 40

role of, 40–42
salary/earnings, 40, 45
skills/personal qualities, 40, 43, 44
training of, 43–44
working conditions, 40, 45
Air Traffic Controller Workforce Plan (Federal Aviation Administration), 42–43, 45
Air Traffic Control System Command Center, 42, 45
Air Traffic Selection and Training exam, 43
Aldrin, Buzz, 63
American Institute for Aeronautics and Astronautics (AIAA), 15, 22–23
American Meteorological Society (AMS), 54
American Physical Society (APS), 15
American Society for Engineering Education (ASEE), 23
AMT Society, 31
Armstrong, Neil, 63
Association of Space Explorers (ASE), 69
Astrogeology Science Center, 62
astronaut, 65
advancement opportunities, 69
certification/licensing, 63
educational requirements, 63, 66
employers of, 67–68
future job outlook, 63, 69
information resources, 69–70
number of jobs, 63
role of, 63–64
salary/earnings, 63, 68
skills/personal qualities, 63, 67
volunteer work/internships, 66–67
working conditions, 63, 68
Astronauts4Hire, 66

aviation/aerospace careers
educational requirements/ salaries, by occupation, 6
number of jobs, 5, 7
See also specific careers
AviationEd, 46
Aviation Institute of Maintenance (AIM), 31
aviation maintenance technical school (AMTS), 27–28, 29
avionics bench techs, 26
avionics technician, 25, 26

Bagenal, Fran, 60
Beutelschies, Guy, 57
Bierman, Elizabeth, 10
Bureau of Labor Statistics (BLS)
on aerospace engineer, 14
on aerospace engineering/ operations technician, 21
on aircraft and avionics equipment mechanic, 30, 31
on air traffic controllers, 46
on commercial pilot, 38

Captain, Tom, 7
Carretero, A. Solé, 57
Cassada, Josh A., 64
Climate Central, 54
commercial pilot, 36
advancement opportunities, 38
certification/licensing, 32, 34
educational requirements, 32, 33–34
employers of, 35
future job outlook, 32, 38
information resources, 38–39
number of jobs, 32
role of, 32–33
salary/earnings, 32, 37
skills/personal qualities, 32, 34–35
working conditions, 32, 36–37

Connolly, John, 9
Connolly, Ron, 42, 45

Department of Defense, US, 5, 12
designated airworthiness
    representative (DAR), 25, 27
Division for Planetary Sciences
    (DPS), 62
Dreier, Casey, 61
drones. *See* unmanned aerial
    vehicles

Engineers Without Borders, 15

Federal Aviation Administration
    (FAA), 25, 46–47
    Airmen Certification, 19
    air traffic controllers hired/
        trained by, 42–43, 45
    on inspection authorized
        mechanics, 26–27
    licensing/testing of pilots by,
        32–33, 34, 35
    regulation of aircraft/avionics
        equipment mechanics by, 27–29
Federal Aviation Administration
    (FAA)/Aviation Careers, 46–47
Flying (magazine), 25
Fresh AJ Weather Blog, 53
Fundamentals of Engineering
    exam, 12

Heldmann, Jennifer, 58–59

*Inspection Authorization
    Information Guide* (Federal
    Aviation Administration), 26–27
inspection authorized (IA)
    mechanics, 25, 26–27
International Astronautical
    Federation (IAF), 62
International Society of Women
    Airline Pilots, 39

International Space Station (ISS),
    5, 64, 65, 66, 68

Jain, A.J., 53
Jensen, Steve, 10
Jet Propulsion Laboratory, 59
Jones, Trevor, 13
Juno space probe, 56–57
just-in-time (JIT) delivery, 54

Kammerer, Doug, 49–50

Lifehacker (website), 10, 32, 33, 37
Lunar and Planetary Institute, 59

Manno, Chris, 32, 33, 37
Mars One, 67–68
Mason, Barbara, 21–22
McClain, Anne, 64, 65, 66
Meir, Jessica, 64
meteorologist
    advancement opportunities, 53
    certification/licensing, 48, 50
    educational requirements, 48, 50
    employers of, 51–52
    future job outlook, 48, 53–54
    information resources, 54–55
    number of jobs, 48
    role of, 48–49
    salary/earnings, 48, 53
    skills/personal qualities, 48,
        49–50, 51
    volunteer work/internships, 50
    working conditions, 48, 52–53
Moroni, Leo, 25, 28
Musk, Elon, 4

NASAPeople: Astronaut Selection
    Program, 70
NASA Quest! (website), 58–59
National Aeronautics and Space
    Administration (NASA), 5, 9, 12,
    51, 61

Astronaut Corps, 64, 66, 68
Pathways Programs, 59
recruitment efforts for astronaut
  candidates, 69
National Air Traffic Controllers
  Association (NATCA), 47
National Center for Aerospace &
  Transportation Technologies, 29
National Centers for
  Environmental Prediction
  (National Weather Service), 51
National Gay Pilots Association
  (NGPA), 39
National Severe Storms Laboratory
  (NSSL), 54–55
National Space Society (NSS), 70
National Weather Service (NWS),
  49, 50, 55
NEXRAD (National Weather
  Service), 51

Occupational Outlook Handbook
  (Bureau of Labor Statistics), 74
Orange County Register, 21–22
Orion deep-space exploration
  vehicle, 69

Pathways Program (National
  Weather Service), 50
Planetary Science Institute (PSI),
  62
planetary scientist
  advancement opportunities, 61
  certification/licensing, 56
  educational requirements, 56, 59
  employers of, 60
  future job outlook, 56, 61
  information resources, 62
  number of jobs, 56
  role of, 56–59
  salary/earnings, 56, 60–61

skills/personal qualities, 56, 59–60
  volunteer work/internships, 59
  working conditions, 56, 60
Planetary Society, 70
Pollitt, Julie A., 9
Popular Mechanics, 52
Principles and Practice of
  Engineering exam, 12
professional engineer (PE), 12

salary/earnings
  for aviation/aerospace careers, by
    occupation, 6
  See also specific occupations
Scientific and Engineering Student
  Internship Program, 59
Society of Women Engineers
  (SWE), 15
SpaceX, 4
Stern, Ted, 71–73
Sutton, Emily, 52
system troubleshooters, 26

thermodynamics, 9

unmanned aerial vehicles (UAVs),
  10, 22
*US Aerospace & Defense Labor
  Market Study*, 7

Virts, Terry, 65
Virtual Air Traffic Simulation
  Network (VATSIM), 47

Washington Post, 50
Women in Aviation International
  (WAI), 23
Women in Planetary Science (blog),
  60

Yoon, Joe, 11–12

Picture Credits

6: Accurate Art, Inc.

11: Shutterstock.com/pressmaster

28: iStockphoto.com/andresr

36: Depositphotos/carlosphotos

65: NASA

About the Author

Stuart A. Kallen is the author of more than 350 nonfiction books for children and young adults. He has written on topics ranging from the theory of relativity to the art of electronic dance music. In addition, Kallen has written award-winning children's videos and television scripts. In his spare time he is a singer, songwriter, and guitarist in San Diego.